INTRODUCTION OF
Re-Ultraexistcreatology, Re-Obirthology

RE — A   RE — U

RE   OBS:

Father, Professor, Reverend, Dr. A. J. Ultraexistcreatologist

Order this book online at www.trafford.com
or email orders@trafford.com

Most Trafford titles are also available at major online book retailers.

Print information available on the last page.

ISBN: 978-1-4251-1408-4 (sc)

Because of the dynamic nature of the Internet, any web addresses or links contained in this book may have changed since publication and may no longer be valid. The views expressed in this work are solely those of the author and do not necessarily reflect the views of the publisher, and the publisher hereby disclaims any responsibility for them.

Any people depicted in stock imagery provided by Thinkstock are models,
and such images are being used for illustrative purposes only.
Certain stock imagery © Thinkstock.

Trafford rev. 09/29/2015

www.trafford.com
North America & international
toll-free: 1 888 232 4444 (USA & Canada)
fax: 812 355 4082

Table Of Contents

✝

Dear miss. mrs. michel Adams:

I'am sending: I' need to send to you the author satisfino money check to pay for the rest of the publishing for the proofs Book Revising printer for I have it written. Two Hundred and twentyfive dols; check.

For the protext Bopton I need these pages to be published.

My Father's name> Angelus Raitzo; mothers name: christalina Kara, Erna Rosalin; my mother died before my Father in Europe. I'am crying, also.

①
② Re-psycho plan to lights / Re-psycho planet to lights in / for the Day, night, and outer spaces, also. / Visited St. Peter, Square Basilica,
Age 2 yrs, The Vatican o, Rome. Almost going on the

Add to Protexto Books:

Re-oBirtholoGods † Re-HolyRe-courtesies:

Int   About The Protexto Books:
Re-oBirthologies (pias), Ultra

use Analysis; concern;
to and, to Be very/very careful of Re-oBirtholoGods
and Re-Devillian Gods
Returning to ReLifes After a Re-deathologist to mean
Skills

All Becomes Re-HolyRe-Angels of the next
Re-Creationgies with Re-Holy Re-Angels a wings;
All should Controlling god Re-oBirtholoGods.
To Be without Re-evils Nos.
All Beings thing Been Beings set up/down
to face Re-eternal Re-fires
Rewards, punishment, psychologies, Fatal-Blow
and pleasures of Re-Devillian Gods
dippers, the dippers of the Stars Days/nights
all are Re-oBirtholoGods, because of doing
Ny kind of evils and Re-evils.
all are going to Be Aware why All thinks that
ways. The only to Think and the Bodies dress Re-will

Re-apostle of Gods
Re-Holy Re-Halo-ologicisms
Re-Holy Re-Priest-ologicisms
Re-psycho existential ogistories, (toriano)
Re-psycho plantology
1) - psycho pl metal ogy
Re-object ology existential psycho plantologisticisms
Re-Birth ologisticisms
ologisticisms
Re-Holy Re-Halo-ologies
Re-Holy Re-crying-ology...
Re-Holy Re-Halo ologies, Re-Nuns, nones/nons
Re- Holy Re-Halo ologoversions
Re-Holy Re-frightfuls-ology / Re-popes-ology
Re-Holy Re-Ancient ology / Re-Holy Re- Re-memory ology
Re-Holy Re-saints ology / Re-Holy Re- Romes ology
Re-Holy Re-lives ology / Re-Holy Re-peace-ology,
Re-Holy Re-freedom ology / Re-Holy Re-Jews ology
Re-Holy Re-Rome ology / Re-Holy Re-Italology
Re-Holy Re-Sanctu-ology, Re-Holy Re-Italiology
Re-Holy Re-Romanos Re-Holy Re-catholology,
Re-Holy Re-Christians Re-Holy Re-catholics
Re-Born's aquinas
Re-so many short/long
Re-terms/Re-concepts
for the protest...
torians
torious
toriano

Re-psycho plntologisticisms

Placed concepts/model to Alter; Table of contents
Re-Jews and Allow to Re-Jews;
Re-Believe and Allow to Re-Believe;
Re-Lives and Allow to Re-Live Re-lifes...
I Am serious Re-tardings, Re-tardo...

Re-HM Re-psych-contesior
Re-.. ; .. - ; -Century
Sincerely yours

All Return to Re-Life/Re-ologies/
Re-concepts/Models of the Re-Birth of Gods

place concepts
models author
the table of contents

†

Re-ologies

Re-ontologies

Re-Birth of Gods

For the Probes
Books from back
pages theo articles and
notes

A/4

Re-Holy Re-prayers
Re-Holy Re-studies; Re-Holy
fasting

Existology

Re-Holy Re-prayers no-plant to versios

Re-Altar poly create existology
Re-Birth poly exist create ology plant to versios
Re-Holy Re-musicals ology versios
Re-Holy Re-musicals - ology versios

For/to Re-Protest afate—Re-Holy Re-cost 1994
All have logics; Re-logically,
Re-Logics, illogics and Re-illogicals,
Re-Orthodologics and Re-devilish logics;
Re-Holy Re-Angels; Re-Holy Re-Jesus
Christ conversions — Amen. Amen.
Re-Holy Re-psycho-Platonic conversions
controllings; Non-controllings, Re-contri
llings; non-Re-controllings By Re
devilish logics also - Amen Amen
Re-psycho-painology, Re-Fatal Blows; Re-etter
Nelfired — Next, All To For the
ception of the Re-Breaks-Protests and Re-con
The Holy Re-christians and the Re-Holy
Re-Catholics; Amen,
Re-Holy Re-Angel conversions
Re-crucifixion of Re-creation Jesus —
Re-Itralogical; — 3 atoms; All aretta
Re-Born, Re-Obirth, Re-again,
Re-natings, Re-fifer after Re-Death
ologies; Also TO/for never endings
of Re-fallings into Infinitudes
Re-Infinities Re-All

Re-little painant deathogies
All been lexical by Re-devilish Godse
Re-Rules; Re-obos Rules, Systems,
systems Rules, Schools, Re-obos Re-obos Re-obos
Re-Rules, also Re-Alphabetic Re-point
All Re-blessings, going Re-Holy to be
evils Re-evils Re-un-natural Blood Re-evil
of Re-devilish Gods — Re-Holy Re-content Jesus Re-series,

✝

A brief Biography of
Re-Fr.Prof.Rev.Dr.A.X.Re-   utterexisttreatologist.
Date of Birth. 01/25/1952. Place of Birth North we
Italy. My Real Familias name are
Ra-i+-zo and Rosalini.,

  My twin Sister died After Birth 01/25/
1952 de Italy. orphahages il
been with at the Age almost going on
two years old. Came to America on a ship.
Phila, PA is not my Real place of Birth.
To old for High Schools and Jr. High Schools
1972   1969

        I'have no one to Help I or turn to.
I'am born a Re-Roman of Re-Cathology
de Italy. I'have enemies in Italy,
America and other countries of Re-oBirthology ods.

✝

A Brief Description The Re-Introduction
of Re-ultraexistreuology, Re-oBirthology,
Re-psycho-plantology, Re-psycho-planetology
Re-ultrapolyexistcreulogies
Re-ultrapolyexist sea-psycho-plantologies — of Planettry
Re-oBirtholo Gods / Re-oBirthologisticgous
crystaliz etholeule Sa-tel-lights. Re-Holy-jesuschrist

Re-Holy Re-prayers; Re-Holy Re-studies;
Re-Holy Re-fastings…, of Re-oBirtholo GODS.
   Furthermore, Beings runs, take chances,
or to tell the truths.
   All Re-ultrapolyexistcreulpsycho-plantological-i-
zations are to Help, and be Help of self and
mother's, andother's…
   Returnings Re-lifes after deaths, Re-Born
agains of Re-oBirtholo Gods. Re-Holy Re-
consearchingovn Re-Holy Re-conforntations of
Re-oBirtholo Gods, Also.

Re-Devillgh Gods Re-psycho-Satanicus / † Re-oBirtholo Gods!
Re-Demon Re-oBirtholumpolars:
Re-Holy Re-Sanctiff-ology! Re-Philestology(etc etc) * θ θ θ /
Re-Frightful-ology Re-Death-ology Re-oBirthology!
Re-Holy Re-Saintology Re-Holy Re-Ghostology!
Re-Holy Re-Soulsology Re-Holy Re-Freedomsology
Re-Holy Re-Ancientology Re-psychoplanthoversos!
Re-Holy Re-Spiritology Re-psycho-Societies
Re-Holy Re-Italiology Re-albomaticus:
Re-Holy Re-Romeology (Shall Be marriages)
Re-Holy Re-Uttragoly...
Re-oBirth...Great psychoplantology / Re-Holy Re-Sucesology
Re-Holy Popesology! Re-Holy Re-Sucesology
Re-Holy Re-Catholic Re-Holy Re-Spiritology!
Re-Holy Re-Christ...ology Re-psychoplantoversities
Re-Holy Re-priest-Christianology
Re-Holy Re-angelumsologists (todos) (Gijo)

His Holiness, Pope Francis
Trafford Publishing, Ph. 1-888-232-4444
1663 Liberty Drive, Bloomington, In.
47403 Re-Holy Re-Dreamsology
Re-multi psycho-Behaviors / Re-Holy psycho-
personalities... Re-Holy Re-Spiritology!
Re-psycho-Societies! Sincerely yours,
Re-Fr. Prof. Rev. Dr. A.J. Re-
Re-Holy Re-Christiano utterexistreatologist (♂) also
Delaware House: 43 Fern Lane, Ancora, New Jersey
08031 Re-Faithology! Re-priestologists, etc etc etc
Re-Holy Re-Dreamsology ISBN13 978-1-4251-14084
Returning as Re-Lifeafter & Deathologists! ID. 185736
Re-Holy Re-Spiritos

Re-Holy Re-
Protext & Book

1988-89. Re-Alkmene

Re-
Holy Re-Jesus christ crystallizethologodethlights/
Re-Holy Re-Magicaloology/
" — " " miracale-ology/
Mysteriology/
Re-Holy-Re-psychgiit crystallizethology la devethlights/
memorology/
Re-psycho-socerios

Re-Holy-Re-courtesy.
Re-Dreams-o-logy/
Re-Holy-Re-courtesaan.
Re-Holy-Re-Priesthology/   (gestieriaan/ frien)
Re-Holy-Re-Cardinalology
Re-Holy-Re-Angeluvaologisaroas
Re- Holy Re-Cardinalology/

Re-Holy-Re-Romanos-Re-Holy-Re-Catholoversioa/
Re-Holy-Re-Romanos-Re-Holy-Re-Cathology/
Re-churches, Re-collegiums, Re-Temples, Re-Synagogues,
Re-Jews-ology, Re-Holy-Re-Faithology, Re-Holy-Re-Cathedrals/
Re-Holy-Re-Institutions, Re-Holy-Re-Constitutions,
Re-universities/ Re-diplomaticus.
Holy/Re-Holy- means to BewellwithoutEvils etc.
Re-Holy-Re-Angeluvaologisas Re-Holy-Re-psycho-Socerios....etc.

Re-White, pink, yellow, orange, Red, Brown and Black till Giants Gorillas
Re-diplomaticus.
originally, Re-aBirthology created, Re-Creating white tall
Giants Gorillas first, circling on Re-aBirthology palms -Re-Suns+
psychoplanets   The Earths   my twin sister died -25/1752/Suns/planets
(Re-metaphysica) D θ θ θ ---
yards between oceans Re-captiious? Re-Holy-Re-Angeluvaologistorios/
Re-psycho planetoloversos, (siss) (oloversities)
Re-psycho plant my twin birth died 01-25-1751-Italy
001 shall spelling of words; Re-social psychology/ Re-aBirth poly-
plantological-i-zations   spells Re-Holyocity concepts-etc.
Re-Holy-Re-Romanos Re-Holy-Re-cathologios/

Re-psycho Exorcistologists
Innocents vs Innocents; Innocents vs Guilty; Guilty vs Innocents; Guilty vs Guilty of

Re-psycho satanicus: Re-Devilish Gods
Re-oBirth polyexist creat psycho plantoloversios:
Un-natural ~~████~~ History Universal christians
In-re-lap-so-Therapies

Un-naturals: Deathologies, creatifications,
oBirthologistifications. Truthologies, lying
Truthologies, Accursios of the un-natural
Accurses, itologies, (un-natural things).

Re-powers/non-re-powers of logics of Re-oBirtholo Gods

Re-powers/non-Re-powers of logics and illogics
of Re-Devilish Gods | Re-Elephyings Re-Elephants without
~~Spindles of plants Also~~ | evils.

Male plants bears male plants; female plants
bears males and females plants during
spring, summer, Fall and winter seasons of
all species and ~~██████~~ outer spaces species
as ~~████~~ so etc. | Re-psycho defensios
                        | Re-psycho camoflages, of Re-Devilish Gods.
                                               Re-psycho confussios
                                               Re-psycho-deprezzios
Re-Idomeology; Re-Idomiology
creates, Re-Creates, Re-duplicates and Re-generates
re-whats so evers re-forevers. Also.
All Seacreatures, land creatures and outer spaces creatures
consumed airs, water, Rains, Fruits and
vegetables also and others as so.
My father was an Italian and my mother was an Italia,
Spanish and Gypsy also of Re-oBirtholo Gods...
I was and still is a born of Rome, ~~Italy~~ Italy.
need to re-correctos of Birth... Amen. Birth Jan/25/1952.

Print these words in The (Protext) Book! or put this in Book also

may you Please Read the back of this page also.

Re-Spiritology / Re-name-ology

Re-Italy / Re-Romes / Re-Angels

Re-Divines-Devoltions Re-Angels

Alphabets Backwards:

ZY: Zatures, XW: christians whites, words,

waters and wisdoms, VUTS: Volts,

(Re-powers / non-re-powers), RQ: Righteous

Quations, PONM: Poetologists,

LK: Likes, JI: Juices, HG: Highests,

FE: Feeds, DC: The-Those and Those

BA: Babies. Re-A/G Re-OBs. History Re-A/U Re-OBs. christians

Re-Lap-so-Therapies of Re-OBirthologbeds

Re-Holy Symbolicals behaviors, Signs,

~~languages~~ languages, and Rituals.

Billions a centuries ago All lived to be

five thousand years of ages, (young children in old

bodies) and other 3price+) species, (creatures)

The Three founders of Re-ultracreatology An

Italian (1), Foster Dunlap (2) and André Robinson (3)

Universal

Christians

Religion

Education

Law

Art

Philosophy

Science

Organization

Therapy of Obirthologod/Obirthologods of these/those Ultrapolyexistcreatologies

(Obirthologies) Amen

Re-Holy Prayers / Re-Holy Studies
...To Be without evils Also...

...All and others than/then All of us All also...

...charismatic orgasmic Intro-Sexual Gratifications levels also...

Universal christians Religion; Education, Law, Art,

philosophy, Science, organization, Therapy of

oBirthologod / OBirthologods etc. Amen. | psychoplanets

Re-oBirth poly exist creat psychoplantological-i-zations | Rotates also.

Re-Ultra " " " " " | Re-psycho creatology

Re-Altra " " " psychoplanetological-i-zations | Re-psychoexistology

Re- Existology, Ultraexistology, Ultracreatexistology, Ultrabiocreatexistology)

" - Createxistology, Ultrapolycreatexistology

Re-multi-psychopersonalities; Re-oBirthiolo Gods /

Re-Devilish Gods and All of us All, and others than/then

All of us All also etc.

...En powers and non-powers of Illogics of Re-Devilish Gods also..

In the beginning God created perfection of creation of the earth and the universe. Nature taking care of nature in motion of God's spirals. Ultraexistcreatology of God created for our nature a long time ago.

The perfection and sensitivity of the nature of God's creation on and of our planet (meaning obirtholumpolar).

God created the heavens, (the sun and the moon, et cetera), earth, people, animals, insects, creatures, air, water, grass and trees perfect and independent of doing what God allows to be done of them, meaning nature working together after God's creation independently: Such as God spoke to all life which God himself created.

The heavens would rain when the trees, grass, flowers, people, animals, insects, and earth needs to drink or to shower themselves in. The day would come when God allows the light to warm us and gave light to see what God created. When life of God became hungry the plants would survive off of the air, rain, water, and soil of God according to their power of God given and man, animals, insects, creatures and organisms survived off of the vegetation given from God to eat during winter and summer weather.

The plants knew when people, animals, insects, creatures, and organisms needs food from them because that was the way God saw life to be. Such as nature taking care of nature of God.

When the morning came, man, animals, insects, creatures, flowers, grass, organisms and trees awoke during the morning and sleep at night.

This was the transition of God's creations in harmony.

The earth was perfect to live walking and running around the very large earth. The land circled the globe in between the waters and the land in between the waters which also circled the earth. Once perfect of God, but the devil destroyed the atmosphere and the earth, man, animals, insects, creatures, grass, trees, flowers, and organisms became petrified and confused also after the destruction.

All ultraexistCreatologists in those Heavens, land/water consumed air, water, Fruits/vegetables in space/outer space as well; and all ultraexistCreatologists are spiritually intelligent or with spiritual intelligenc

note: various types of powers etc. Amen. There are two factors involving ours/their Creations: The Universal christians R.E.-L.A.P.-S.O-Therapy of God/Gods. Amen. OBirtholoGod/OBirtholoGods Also. Amen. And also, The Un-natural universal christians Ur-R.E.-L.A.P- S.O.-Therapy of Devilish God/Devilish Gods. Amen.

meaning they are indestructible to themselves and foreverlasting forever of/in those ultra poly-existCreatologies, (OBirthologies). Amen. Countless infinities that go on forever/yeu goes Amen.

The purpose of teaching this Science is
to enrich and to inform a class (body of
students) of what GOD means of creation.
This is what ultraexistcreatology is based
on. *Now the sun runs from the th the now*
focus none until the eclipse comes. Amen.

O birth old m polar! All planeta only during
the daytime of ancient beginning of this/first around
in creation before our future. Amen.

The Belief of Ultraexistcreatology

The Belief in Ultraexistcreatology consist of being either monotheism or Polytheism, as one and many of Obirthologods, people, animals, insects and creatures (Air, Water, Fruits, Vegetalbles etc.) may believe in or of the Ultrapolyexistcreatology in Jesus Christ's name. Amen.

What ever Obirthologod(s) have us to believe in or of then we believe in and act as accordingly of the test in trials/tribulations differently of experiences effectively of our/in our Un-Natural nature.

The belief of Ultraexistcreatology is the Universal Christians Religion, Education, Law, Art, Philosophy, Science, Organization, and Therapy righteously without evils. Amen.

originally: ozone+apeebiousreptameeto: oBirthologods. Amen.
Crystalize Globeof Satellites: oBirthologods. Amen. ⚗

* Idoneologies: oBirthologod/oBirthologods has/have always been here until oBirthologod/oBirthologods creates/created oBirthologod/oBirthologods themselves and others etc. Amen.

* Idomiologies: oBirthologod/oBirthologods creates/created and creating others and there/their are others (oBirthologod/oBirthologods besides oBirthologod/oBirthologods in which oBirthologod/oBirthologods has/have not created etc. Amen. Spontaneous/Simultaneous creatifications foreverlasting/nonforeverlasting etc. Amen. also in and of trans transitionally etc Amen. Bless all of us and us all in Jesus christs name. Amen.

The memorial in Jesus Christ's name. Peace, Love, Truth,/Freedom to you/all of us.
There are various types of Student Class Graduate (Collegiums) Governments, and most
of them/those Universal Christians Religion, Education, Law, Art, Philosophy, Science,
Organization, and Therapy of Obirthologod(s) Amen., are in and of Memorial of Jesus
Christ (Universal prayers/Studies) of all ologies that ends with these letters ology;
and that also, with a prefix/suffix together for instance, the word Ultrapolyexistcreatolog.
(Obirthology) is a Memorial in Jesus Christ's name of learning from Obirthologod(s). Amen.,
also. Courtesy: Respecting all/everyone's belief. Collegiums (churches/colleges)

Gospel(s) of Ultraexistcreatology (Obirthology) of and for Obirthologod(s) and
those Ultraexistcreatologist(s) in Jesus Christ's name. Amen.
OcomeHapcebiousreptameets. Amen. Bless all of those Ultrapolyexistcreatologists/
Obirthologods and others besides us as well. Amen So may Peace, Love, Truth/Freedom
be in Jesus Christ's name of Obirthologods. Amen.

Sing praises of Divine pure righteousness throughout and around those Heavens/
Universes (Obirtholoverses) to Obirthologods. Amen. For they shall listen to you/all
within faith/(Truthology) as well. For there are many creatifications here, various,
as well as out there or throughout there of those universes; and there are also an
infinitive amount forever of those Obirthologod(s) Amen.

Sing praises to those Heavens where Obirthologod(s) dwell every day/night for
all of us here (The living/the dead for all Ultraexistcreatologists as purily well).
For Obirthologods watch forever/endurance forever all together. Amen.

Pray prayers forever, forever peace, love, truth/freedom to/for all throughout
the Universal Christians Religion, Education, Law, Art, Philosophy, Science, Organization,
Therapy of Obirthologods. Amen.

May Obirthologod(s) bless all of these/those Ultraexistcreatologists and Bless

Obirthologod(s) in Jesus Christ's name.   Amen

Then we have the un-natural universal
christians M.R.E.-L.A.P.-S.O.-Therapy of Devilish God/
Devilish Gods. Amen.

The unnatural universal christians
M-R.E.-L.A.P.-S.O.-Therapy of Devilish God/
Devilish Gods. Amen.

Sincerely yours,

Prof. Rev. Dr. A.L. Ultraexist-
creatologist(s)

Preface

Time to Speak When Only Directed by God

These are one of many of God's newest and oldest
original philosophies as well as God's powers of beauty being
and been originally an exotically approached and described
by only those who recognize these ancient creatologies, en-
lightened by God. Saying and said in prayer by our God as
a musician, poet, philosopher, artist, dancer, preacher and
the teacher up and around the high heaven all alone, by
himself long ago. God had not a family of Gods until God
created them, and neither was their a family of our particular
species, etc.

The philosophies and knowing the philosophies which
also describes God's beautiful powers which bring knowledge.
God regenerates, reduplicates and recreates himself of his
own Godly powers. God is never alone because God has a
family of their particular nature also well known as the God
family or Godly family of the high heavens as well as God's
creates and created us of opposite sex to reproduce a given
family of our own particular species as well as to be under-
stood. Amen.

The Original Founder and Discoverer is

Anthony Jessie Williams of

the First Five Developmental Phenomenons

of These Particular Philosophical Introspections

and Treatise of Classification

CREATOLOGY: means prayer and study of God's creations such as animals, insects, creatures, trees, plants and mankind. It also means a particular phenomenon which creates only a phenomenon, but does not exist to create this typical phenomenon. Amen.

EXISTCREATOLOGY: prayer and study of God's existence which became of creation (air, water and the earth); and insects, creatures, trees, plants and mankind's existence which also became of creations of God within themselves such as birth creators and plucking of vegetables from the Garden of Eden during the first Genesis. Life on earth exists to create such as dancing, singing, talking, walking, eating, drinking pure water. Amen. (Certified since October 23, 1976 by ULC, Inc.)

ULTRAEXISTCREATOLOGY: means prayer and study beyond existence of God's creation and beyond the existence which became God's creation. It also means nature which is their own time of such given existences of God's creations such as plants, trees, insects, creatures, animals and mankind. Amen. (Certified since April 15, 1980 by ULC, Inc.)

ULTRABIOEXISTCREATOLOGY: means prayer and study beyond the two existences which became of life's two creations. It also means beyond two existences which became God's creation. Amen.

ULTRAPOLYEXISTCREATOLOGY: means a prayer and study beyond many existences which became of God's creation and also means beyond many existences which became of God's many creations. There are also many creations which are interrelated with God which are positive and others which are non-related with God because they are probably negative or either unknown to one another or living beyond many existences which became their particular species of creation or either acting-out against one another among their own kind. It also means beyond the ultimate of many of life's existences which became of many creations of God. Amen.

iv

Prayer and study were never necessity until evil became as of destruction or either according to the Holy Bible, St. Mark, Chapter 1 verse 13. God is also responsible for creating such evil in animals, insects, creatures, trees, plants, as well as man. God's behavior is not relatively responsible for what he himself does. Amen.

An ultraexistcreatologist is one who prays, studies and interprets beyond the existence of God's creation, and it also means a branch of prayer and study concerned with natural observation and pure classification of facts with the establishment of variable, specific and general laws of the universe of God. Amen.

The first law and experimental reasoning of the first five developmental phenomenons of these particular introspections and treatise of classificantion are to enjoy rather than destroy any being of existence (life) which became of creation or many creations of life from God. Amen.

In God we belove, believe and trust but the Devil corrupts our souls universally.

Note: Born to know knowledge rather than of prayer and study. God creates and created all of knowing the same knowledge or to know the identical perceptons of life, but instead the Devil attacks and marks all with misunderstandings towards one another.

About God of Ultraexistcreatology

God has no beginning or no ending of himself.

God has been here since his own creation and before his very own being without form meaning: spiritual ultrapoly-existcreatrons and obsreptameetrons which means formless magnetic being or beings of the same or not of the same body, created from himself, which also means spirit or spirits of God. Amen.

God's name is according to ocomehapcebiousreptameets or ocomehapcebiousreptameetrons which means O I say O come O I lovegtables O I say O come have happen and been sent by all of us religion, education, preacher, teacher, association, meets which means also obsreptameets.

God changes from one being to another of himself. God can make his Godly being mental, ultrapolyexistcreatological, metaphysical or physical to be beyond or not at all of the beyond to create the same as for to exist of himself.

God remains supreme of ultra or altra powers. God is superior over all or not over all--if God wishes to remain so, just being or not a being at all, but only to be of the beyond existence of many creations of God himself. Very powerful source or no source at all. What I mean is this: God can be what ever to be, God can or shall be and do. God made himself infinity to exist to create. God is almighty.

This science was created by God, brought down or up to

man as an ultraexistcreatologist.   Amen.   Given to man to be
an ultraexistcreatologist.

The Revelation and characteristics of what God is like
of the beyond existence of creation follow:

God is a spirit, a spirit without form of himself which
has no beginning or ending or no beginning or ending of God
himself.   God is also a spirit without life and without death
of himself and others which God creates or created other than
us.

God is lifeless but with life.

God is infinity which is also undestructable to himself
and with existing to create other then to create form for
himself.

God is also colorless or with color--if God desires to
create for himself, or at sometimes which he does.

God is senseless, but with sense of perception.

God is superior of intelligence.

God is clear to see or sense.

God is clear like the color clear, but of infinity very
powerful also solid.

God's organism is made undestructable too.

Abovenessnesses: OBietholoGod/OBirtholoGods
also etc., UltrapolyexistCreatologies, (OBirthologies),
Idomiologies / Idomeologies indestructabilities
UltrapolyexistKreatrons/OBirthrons: Crystalized Globeof Satel-
-lights also. Amen.

Primarily Original Prayers and Studies of God
In Ultraexistcreatology

You will find that there are three types of prayer and study.

1. Personal Prayer (known as private prayer) consists of praying to or for oneself of God.

2. Social Prayers (known as schools, churches, colleges or institutions praying collectively).

3. Universal Prayer (known as natural praying to God and for the universe of God one or many praying to God and all of God's creations).

1. Personal Study (consists of private study without interference of others and God).

2. Social Study (consists of a class of people working together of God. Learning identical knowledge).

3. Universal Study (consists of all the evidence of knowledge learned of God and not of God).

Observation of Obirthology

What do the stars and the moon represent or symbolize?
This is what I reveal of God's night-time atmosphere. In
various ways the stars and the moon mean creations' develop-
ments and obirthology from my scientific endeavors, which
means there are a lot more here and everywhere so called
ultrapolyexistcreatologies existing of the infinite skies
(galaxies).

When I or you look at the moon and stars, we receive
the acknowledgements that God means: there are also others
who are creating besides God himself in the universe.

Yes, God covers his territorial creations such as others,
also such as Gods, and the many other ultrapolyexistcreatologies which maintain theirs.

God tells me as an ultraexistcreatologist that He sees
(senses) evil being done to his (our) creation which never
can be avoided of them doing so.

That's one of the reasons why God is weary and avoids
helping our earth and the universe, simply because he is
either busy in creating other creations or the Devil and
Devils (others-while Gods) are intefering with ours so that's
why God is ignoring and has kept silence toward his creation;
sometimes remaining hidden, because evil is being done to
us and God also of the ultrapolyexistcreatologies.

What is God like and where is God or why are we not

like God?

First of all I would like to explain what God is like: God is a supreme being of all the universe and life. God is the ruler and creator of all beings, things, himself.

God is consistent of one or more spiritual personalities because, of his creatings God creates in what he feels what's needed.

The reason why I say this is because, as an ultraexist-creatologist, I find that what we experience here on earth and throughout the universe are the multitudes of creations with differences and variations of perceptions, feelings, emotions, creativities and life's performances.

What I sense in God I also sense in the earth among people, animals, creatures, trees and the universe.

What I mean is this, God's feelings are in us as a creation. Feelings which come from God created in us.

This is why we acknowledge God in various ways and believe in God despite changes and differences of our own convictions.

What I mean is this: God creates in various ways, and in various ways many of us have come to accept or believe in him (God).

Second of all, where is God?

God lives in his own universe and lives within himself (other than ours). What I mean is this: God has a place where God lives free in himself and his universe (kingdom of

Heaven).

Furthermore, God can be anywhere throughout the entire universe of in general terms many places everywhere.

Conclusion: Why are we not like God?

The reason why lives like us remain unlike God is because God anticipated on how his creations should and shall be. Was it that God became frightened of what he might have (sensed first) created?

Was it that God is only capable of creating what he can?

Or is it that God is very jealous of us becoming Gods like our God himself (of the same omnipotent nature).

The reason why we have not become Gods like God is because God created us to know that we can or shall never be Gods like God himself, because of what we experience here such as evils will only cause the total destructions of the ultrapolyexistcreatologies (space, the universe, planets, infinities, other Gods and existences) to occur dangerously among each other.

This is one of the reasons why we can not become Gods, because God also fears danger among what he can create.

This is one example on earth of how we shall never be Gods. Because God fears the powers to create could be created in others than us to be like himself.

From a very powerful source such as God why couldn't we be like him, of that same source when even we are to remain inferior while God remains supreme of all. The almighty, the powerful Godly source we were created from, but in creation God has only degraded us and caused us to be of less powers of all life like us; inferior to God and what He creates and others besides God himself.

What causes God/Gods to create, recreate, these/those ultrapolyexist Creatologies, (OBirthologies?).

Why do Devilish God/Devilish Gods can never avoid doing evils (un-natural Deathologies also? Amen.; Pains/Sufferings, trials/tribulations.

* OBirtholoGod/OBirtho Gods also. Amen.

What possessed ultrapolyexist Creatologies? Such as indestructibles/foreverlastings meaning; God/Gods; Devil/Devils; also other OBirtholoverses/those ultrapolyexistCreatologies (natural Truthologies/un-natural Truthologies also and others which have been known/un-known to them also. Also. amen.

xii

meaning OBirtholoGod/OBirtholoGods Infinities etc., also on/on always always go on/on infinities. Amen.

Introduction

This book is only designed for higher religious educational sciences. For people and students of non-traditional doctrines and students of non-denominational thought; but only to believe in what is right and absolutely pertinent. Also, this book prepares you with a wide range and scope of details and religious educational scientific speculations, insights, research, rank, laity, refinement and projections.

Attention: Please, there's no need to argue or fight because of what you believe in of ultraexistcreatology when this is an advance fact when you know the other person doesn't believe in what you believe of God. Amen.

Or O Birtholo Gods also. Amen. Models: Parables/Syllables according to perception (+) of moon (a) / Stars. Amen.

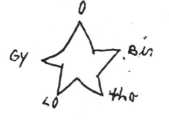

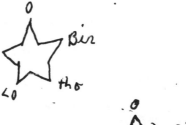

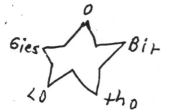

Central Formulation

I am young, and I am getting old as an ultraexist-creatologist. I also have been told by a God and me to be saved of our souls.

In order to build and rebuild this science we need to come to support a concession of being versatile first then concordance, and with our support we will acknowledge all that are of sensory and feedback. Intelligently and spiritually. Amen.

My Search of and for Ultraexistcreatology

Ultraexistcreatology is an idealogical and independable speculation searched by me of my own outstanding entry of self-explorations. In life and the many beyond existences of many creations are my consciousnesses and concerns here for to enchant and to reason with others.

Yes, the science taken a while after I began to find what I am looking for, looking at, and looking with. Knowing all of the time that these are exactly and expectantly to be.

Furthermore, this book will only have knowledge and record to interest and support the readers to do research after my search of the identity and ability of ultraexist-creatology and ultrapolyexistcreatology etcetera.

So after this will only bring forth an enrichment and

accreditation of Science to be again simulated and explored.

Furthermore, ultraexistcreatologies are the all times, all kinds, anywhere, everywhere and so on discussions of life.

My philosophical science of ultraexistcreatology is a divine revelation of God telling me what are the activities and occurances of the universe.

A divine message which explains various beyond existences of God's creations.

I received this divine revelation when I became an ordained minister then an ultraexistcreatologist.

In This Course of Ultraexistcreatology We
Recommend and Supply the Test for Acceptance
of Your and Our Approvals

The Biography of Professor A.J. Ultraexistcreatologist of Obirthologod

I was born in Philadelphia on December 3, 1954. As a child, I grew up learning christian education (born a christian) in and out of my Fathers's/Mother's churches which were of the Baptist and Methodist faiths. They met in Philadelphia on Broad Street and going to Jehovah Services on Sunday. From that experiance, I only learned that the only true universal christians, religion, education, law, art, philosophy, science, organization, and therapy is of Obirthologod and myself which I believe in. Also, after moving to New Jersey, I met my Aunt who attended Mt. Calvery Baptist Church in Camden, New Jersey. I also attended the Holy Catholic Church in Philadelphia and in New Jersey.

I have attended and still attend as long as I shall live the place Obirthologod has for me/us throughout the heavens after I die un-natural death. That is one reason why I pray to Obirthologod. Amen.

I have also in my life taken much critisism as young as I was and being tall for my age since the past and now the future because the devilish God will not let me go.

My christian education is good. I received outstanding improvemtnt taking special classes at Shoemaker Jr. High School in Philadelphia.

I also attended Woodrow Wilson High School in Camden, New Jersey but didnot graduate from the 12th grade and then latter years I was referred to Camden County College and earned 24 college credits to achieve a high school diploma from the state of New Jersey (Board of Education) Later, about in June of 74, I joined the military (U.S.Army). I received a general discharge under honorable conditions for medical reasons.

I came from the U.C.R.E.-L.A.P.-S.O. therapy of all creations of our God. Amen. I also was referred to join the Universal Life Church in California. The Divine Revelation came upon me being because I pray.

This is one of the reasons why and how the Introduction of Ultraexistcreatology came in to being because of prayer. I also learned prayer because of our large family whom we believe in Jesus Christ and as I became an ordained minister through U.L.C., also hearing the Holy Divine words and message of the OB's schools and Ultraexistcreatology studing the creations also of Obirthologods. Amen.

I am also a Disabled American Veteran in which I became injured on duty and accused of wrong in which I did not do.

I was born in Philadelphia on December 8, 1954. As a child, I grew up learning christian education (born a christian) in and out of my Fathers's/Mother's churches which were of the Baptist and Methodist faiths. They met in Philadelphia on Broad Street and going to Jehovah Services on Sunday. From that experiance, I only learned that the only true universal christians, religion, education, law, art, philosophy, science, organization, and therapy is of Obirthologod and myself which I believe in. Also, after moving to New Jersey, I met my Aunt who attended Mt. Calvery Baptist Church in Camden, New Jersey. I also attended the Holy Catholic Church in Philadelphia and in New Jersey.

I have attended and still attend as long as I shall live the place Obirthologod has for me/us throughout the heavens after I die un-natural death. That is one reason why I pray to Obirthologod. Amen.

I have also in my life taken much critisism as young as I was and being tall for my age since the past and now the future because the devilish God will not let me go.

My christian education is good. I received outstanding improvemènt taking special classes at Shoemaker Jr. High School in Philadelphia.

I also attended Woodrow Wilson High School in Camden, New Jersey but didnot graduate from the 12th grade and then latter years I was referred to Camden County College and earned 24 college credits to achieve a high school diploma from the state of New Jersey (Board of Education) Later, about in June of 74, I joined the military (U.S.Army). I received a general discharge under honorable conditions for medical reasons.

I came from the U.C.R.E.-L.A.P.-S.O. therapy of all creations of our God. Amen. I also was referred to join the Universal Life Church in California. The Divine Revelation came upon me being because I pray.

This is one of the reasons why and how the Introduction of Ultraexistcreatology came in to being because of prayer. I also learned prayer because of our large family whom we believe in Jesus Christ and as I became an ordained minister through U.L.C., also hearing the Holy Divine words and message of the OB's schools and Ultraexistcreatolog studing the creations also of Obirthologods. Amen.

I am also a Disabled American Veteran in which I became injured on duty and accused of wrong in which I did not do.

Synopsis or Summary

Ultraexistcreatology is and are the characteristics, naturalistics, and realistics of actual prayer, study and enjoyment around the behavior and distributions of life.

Furthermore, ultraexistcreatology is the study of all behaviors of the universe and others like the Solar System and God.

Theory

God is not perfect because we are not perfect.

This is substantial and leads to belief of this ultra-existcreatological awareness, but I will also be and walk positive in the sight of God regardless of what state God may be within or of.

This is one science that needs to be acknowledged of all perspectives regardless of race, religion, creed, or faith.

I love God, but does God love us? The reason why I say this is because of total destructions.

Definitions

Ultrabioexistcreatology: means prayers and study of the beyond two existences of creation of God; it also means beyond two existences of two creations of God. Amen.

Ultraexistcreatology is strictly a sight seeing phenomenon: such as stars, the moon which means in short terms obirthology, the Solar System, the universe and other many beyond existences of God's creations etcetera. Amen.

Idomiology: means there are other life forms interrelated and non-interrelated among each other through space, and space is a very infinite place according to God and God's people or creations such as Gods and the beyond many existences of many creations. Meaning: God's creations and other than God's creations such as Gods and the infinitive many existences of many creations of them all and their creations. Note: Means all and all and other than others.

Idomeology: Therefore, means God creates and has created God himself and of our particular life forms of birth also, etcetera. This is what the moon and the stars represent: Oh I say, Oh come Oh I lovegetables Oh I say Oh come Holy altrapolycreatexistbirthology, religion, education, preacher, teacher, association, meets; also the Gods and the infinite beyond many existences of many creations and powers.

The conception of God and Gods. The weight and size of them are infinitively and beyond enormous and of various perceptive colors, color rays, and ultimate growth. The powers sort of speak are vivid and sharp of their particular organisms and structures etcetera.

Major Point: Refers to ultrapolyexistcreatology. God creates infinitively of Idomeology and Idomiology. Also in terms there are all types of levels, being and living the beyond existence of creation. God lives beyond many existences of many creations; and God beyond many existences of creations creates various levels and powers of and through the ultrapolyexistcreatologies.

Definitions: Idomeology means God creates and created himself, and us, etcetera.

Ultrapolyexistcreatrons: Means, also, visible and invisible life, energies, powers, levels, circuits, forms, characteristics, and positions, etcetera, of our Idomeological God, and Idomiological God.

God: God is made up of ultrapolyexistcreatrons and obsreptameetrons, meaning God shall only create and recreate of God's own free ultrapolyexistcreatological organisms etcetera.

Note: Oh come Hapcebious means, Oh come have happen and been sent by all of us; only by the Gods and fundamentally speaking by us beings too.

Oh I say Oh come Oh I Lovegetables Oh I say Oh come Hapcebious religion, education, preacher, teacher, association meets. The philosophies of the Gods.

God's Creatings and Drawings in the Air and Clouds

As I see and sense God and God's creatings, drawings and figures of creations in the high clouds--showing and telling me this, "our creations and obirthology (obsrepta-meets) once abundance dying unnatural death," such as the animals, insects, creatures, trees, humans and the one drawing I see done by God of the clouds also look like the devil who had fallen from heaven once an angel, a God of sorts, relating to me also as if I were a devil also.

Yes, such communication and reminiscences do occur even with feelings by God's causes, affects and effects of and towards our nature and others (ultrapolyexistcreatologies).

The Ultrapolyexistcreations doing evil:

* Such as when the sunlight shines life reminds me of hate.

* Such as when the rain falls life reminds me of God and all of ours and nature's tears crying to be saved.

* Such as when the wind blows life reminds me of the nature, but unlike God's--such as life like us, because God only creates and created the air unlike God's breath; and also God makes the winds go against our nature, etcetera.

* Such as when Obirthology (the moon and the stars shine) life reminds me of many others out there besides us whom are also being destroyed and whom acknowledge us.

The Philosophies Which Became of God Through Birth
and of Idomeology and Idomiology (Others)

Oh I say Oh come Oh I lovegetables Oh I say Oh come Hapcebious religion, education, preacher, teacher, association, meets: Oh I Say Oh come Oh I lovegetables Oh I say Oh come have happen and been sent by all of us: which also means, (only by the Gods' which brought us here and others then us also God or Gods).

Oh I say Oh come Oh I lovegetables Oh I say Oh come Holy Altrapolycreatexistbirthology (gy means gigantic in size) religion, education, preacher, teacher, association, meets: OBSREPTAMEETS.

Note: God, Gods and ultrapolyexistcreatologies are of Idomeology and Idomiology.

(A) Definitions:

Obirthology: Means or represents the moon, life, other life forms of birth by other Gods which also creates and also created themselves, the stars of infinities, and many beyond many existences of many creations of Idomiology.

Ultrapolyexistcreatifications: Means, the beyond many or infinities of characteristics and many existences of many creations of God and Gods creating or created life such as us and other then us.

(B) Note: Our God also creates and has created Gods as I mention in this text.

Author's Perspective

To explain and emphasize morals and attributions towards given expectations in our government. My basic concerns are to protect, to support, to help, and to serve the United States as an ultraexistcreatologist of these genuine acknowledgements.

To further my approvals are to investigate, to generate experience and forum.

The Nature of God

The nature of God is this that God became of appearance to create and created self.

God became of Idomeology which means God always has been here until God creates and created himself. God, like magic out of ultrapolyexistcreatology, became of Idomeological birth.

There were also other ultrapolyexistcreatologies after and before our God in the heavens.

Definitions:

Ultradomes: means beyond where all life forms live and God etcetera. Amen.

Death: means an unnatural and illogical being or beings of where no being lives and where no being nonlives at all.

Ultracreatology: means prayer and study of the beyond creations in life, pray and study of God. Amen.

The Messages and (Concepts) Acknowledgements of God and Idomiologies

God created us and there are other Gods and the beyond (all true many existences of many creations) many existences of many creations which also creates and created us: other than us. Meaning, we all are one of many; us in a sense, but differently creating and created of God. Note: God and us are also effected by other ultrapolyexistcreatologies.

Criterion: We all acknowledge God's powers and creativities; also, we are unlike God, but we rather become Gods like them.

This is one of my reasons why I am jealous, because I am not like God as God or Gods like them all of infinities (ultrapolyexistcreatologies).

Introduction to Ultrapolyexistcreatology

(C) Note: Primarily God our God does not know all of the beyond many existences of many creations when there or theirs others besides our God himself, because our God in the ultrapolyexistcreatologies are unlike, unknown (too far away), or like other Gods creations, but never been of creation, creatings, or created by them when our God acknowledges others (more) than just our God himself creating. Meaning and knowing other creations besides himself (God) of which God himself did not do or created. Also viceversa.

The Introduction of Ultraexistcreatology centuries ago, the oceans outside divided by land north/south side sea waters was clear to see all seacreatures as the land rotated inbetween the oceans, but now after the centures distruction became about by Devish Gods, amen.

The seacreatures, once natural/pure air, water, fruits, and vetegetarians before, but in general. Now the seacreatures began attacking one another for for food un-naturally.

Throughout the universe (the ultra poly exist creatologies) obirthologirally were natural/ pure by consuming the air, water, fruits, and vegetables of obirthologods, amen.

Centuries ago obirthorian (man) and Obirthoria (woman) since the very first beginning (Adam/Eve) sort of speak always had worshiped Obirthologod (s).

The reason of he/she worshiping because of the various wonderful powers crea⁺ified by obirthologod, amen.

He/she was once and the generation after them were white tall giant gorrillas consuming only the air, water, fruits, and vetables of Obirthologod, amen. Long ago since the very beginning of creation, amen. at day (morning) time only. Amen. Appeared in the day time creation (s) of OBirth logod (s), Amen. Yellow Sun / white Skies when the morning comes; refered centuries ago. Sun / planets means OBirtholumpolans of OBirtholoGod (s) also. Amen, also, all planets rest at night centuries ago,

Ultraexistcreatology

Ultraexistcreatology of life's natural sense of perception was once beautiful until a Devil destroyed the natureal orders of life here.

Obirthologod and what so ever out there are watching very closely about what life does here, because life here are nothing but accurses of the accurses now.

Ultraexistcreatology is also praying and studing other planets and different types of universes and what cause them universes and others to be created. The prayer and study about Obirthologods behaviors of Gods's self and others out there and beyond out there-here/there.

God's Knowledge of Ultrapolyexistcreatology

(D) The Nature of Authorship is to bring forth knowledge of which was never known or known to God and man, meaning there are others such as ultrapolyexistcreatologies after, before, and simultaneously creating and created of our God and not of our God which God knows and knew of others, just as powerful as our God which have knowledge of and unknown knowledge of other Gods, but knowing also out there, there are others beyond and ultimates of many existences of many creations.

Other Gods and many beyond existences of creations with our God and not with our God which are Gods which our God recognizes. Meaning, there are others besides God himself. For example, not just God and Gods, but also of the beyond many existences of many creations, have never been created by our God which our God knew of.

A revelational proven fact of ultrapolyexistcreatologies but untrue to other opinions, religions, educations, laws, and sciences, etcetera.

This science is to advanced for most people who do not know the ultrapolyexistcreatological spaces and their involvements.

Furthermore, this science needs no documentary research of other scientists, philosophers, poets, theorists, educators, etcetera, because ultraexistcreatology stands alone of life's own intelligent speculative and documentations searched by me.

Another reason why I do not use other peoples' knowledge is because people may think I've stolen someone else's or their ideas to support mine and ours.

Second of all, this science is substantially and voluntarily self supported (proven) by God and me, etcetera.

(E) Important Note:

There are also other Gods of Idomeology or Idomeological birth which means they have created themselves etcetera.

Furthermore, God and the Gods are not like our beyond existence (man) which became of creation from God.

Furthermore, God and Gods are not or neither male or female nor are they neuter.

The Gods consist of obsreptameetrons and ultrapolyexistcreatrons etcetera.

To be invisible, the Gods they are and shall be seen because the Gods are only creating obsreptameetrons and ultrapolyexistcreatrons etcetera.

(F) Important Note:

There are also other Gods of Idomeology or Idomiological birth which means they created themselves and other than of our God's ultrapolyexistcreatologies.

(G) Note: God is beyond intelligence of himself such as one aspect why he creates and created the ultrapolyexistcreatologies.

The reason why? Simply because God creates and created himself to do so but sometimes is irrational or uncontrollable towards creations.

Note: There are also other Gods and ultrapolyexistcreatologies, of Idomeology and Idomiology.

Furthermore, God creates infinitively of Idomeology and Idomiology.

OhIsayohcomeoIlovegetablesohIsayohcomehapcebiousreptameets: means, Oh I say Oh come O I lovegetables Oh I say Oh come holy altrapolycreatexistbirthology religion, education, preacher, teacher, association, meets; Oh I say Oh come Oh I lovegetables Oh I say Oh come have happen and been sent by all of us religion, education, preacher, teacher, association, meets; Obsreptameets. Of only the Gods.

Note: This is an absolute fact that there are Gods because of the above caption.

The field of ultraexistcreatology is also the performance for law, art and science.

For the student who takes a course of this particular curriculum in ultraexistcreatology will and shall be given an option such as to major toward what the student's goals and needs are planned to be.

Such as whether students want to take ultraexistcreatology as either an art or a science or both at the same time--should they consult with their academic advisor for explanations and details before graduation.

So after graduation of Ultraexistcreatology--graduate students will be recognized and accepted for gainful employment according to your interests. Such as wherever you or their conscience allows them to seek may the light be the way of pleasure not evils or violence.

God's gift to men and women etcetera is the information of acknowledging the right and left hand (such as the palms and fingers).

The right and left hand God shows and tells me as an ultraexistcreatologist, Anthony Jessie Williams, Jr., that they mean Idomeology and Idomiology along also with fingers.

How do we or I go about this or proving this: By an example on the diagram below. Two figures of the right and left hand representation: Starting from the top hand drawing which is a picture of the right hand facing front with the baby finger in syllabication along with the second finger then palm, middle finger, index finger and the thumb means Idomeology or Idomiology visa vis. Which means Idomeology; God created himself and us etcetera. Idomiology means other life forms of God, Gods and the beyond many existences of many creations of God and other than Gods etcetera.

Left Hand Paradigm

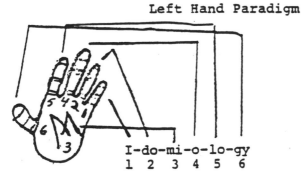

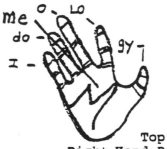

I-do-mi-o-lo-gy
1 2 3 4 5 6

Top
Right Hand Paradigm

The letter "M" in each hand the palm that is representative of me and mi of the philosophy and concepts of God. Originally of these expressions only Idomeology and Idomiology of the hands.

Ultraexistcreatology

As an ultraexistcreatologist, I avail and recommend for this science to be of teachings for student class government; student class graduate government; and (college) all walks of life.

OBSREPTAMEETS

Com-po-sites
and

CAPULAR S

and

RABULAR S

com-po-sites
Cap-u-lars
Ra-bu-lars

The Founder's Feelings of Being and Living of Ultrapolyexistcreatologies and As An Ultraexistcreatologist

I do the best I can to help us, but I do not feel absolutely free in this world. What worries me are evils, conflicts, agony, irony, displacements, the bad, the negative, poison, criminals, jealousy, anger, wars, destructions, curses, witch craft, bad luck, cheaters, the disadvantaged, the lonely, the abused, the hungry, the disabled, misfortuned, abortion, disaster, the blind, the crippled, disease, disorders, malfunction, catastrophe, prostitution, disorganization, abnormal behavior, illogics, disposition, slavery, prejudice, discrimination, hatred, liars, disestablishment, penalties, the Devil, death, etcetera.

Author's Certifications

Certificates of Anthony J. Williams, Jr.

The Universal Life Church, Inc., Modesto, California 95351, Certified Anthony J. Williams, Jr. because of his findings on existcreatology and existcreatologist since 3/14/76 then Certified October 23, 1976, involving a synopsis, etcetera.

High School Diploma, State of New Jersey, Department of Education, May 25, 1977, where I graduated at Trenton, New Jersey.

Doctor of Metaphysics through U.L.C., Inc., Modesto, California 95351 where I attained my degree (corresponded, etcetera).

Also Certified again through U.L.C., Inc. on ultraexistcreatology and ultraexistcreatologist, April 15, 1980, of another synopsis of my own findings.

The author's Certificates are actually connected to the Introduction of Ultraexistcreatology. To show proof that this science is actual and Certificates are valid of approval.

Universal Life Church, Inc.

HEADQUARTERS, 601 3RD ST., MODESTO, CALIF. 95351 • (209) 527-9353 OR 527-8111

This is to certify that ANTHONY J. WILLIAMS

has been granted the title of EXISTCREATOLOGY

by Universal Life Church, Inc. this day   OCTOBER 23, 1976

Kirby J. Hensley
Bishop Kirby J. Hensley, President

Universal Life Church, Inc.

HEADQUARTERS: 601 3RD ST., MODESTO, CALIF. 95351 • (209) 527-0553 OR 527-8111

This is to certify that **Anthony J. Williams**

has been granted the title of **Existereatologist**

by Universal Life Church, Inc. this day **October 23, 1976**

Kirby J. Hensley
BISHOP KIRBY J. HENSLEY, President

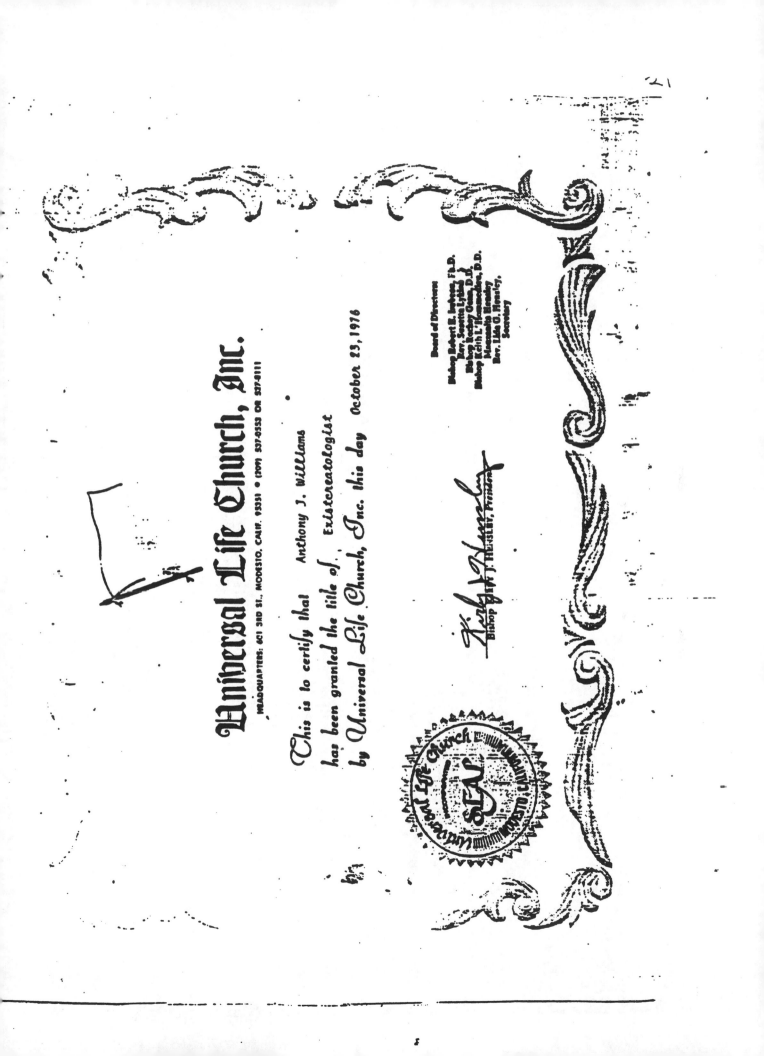

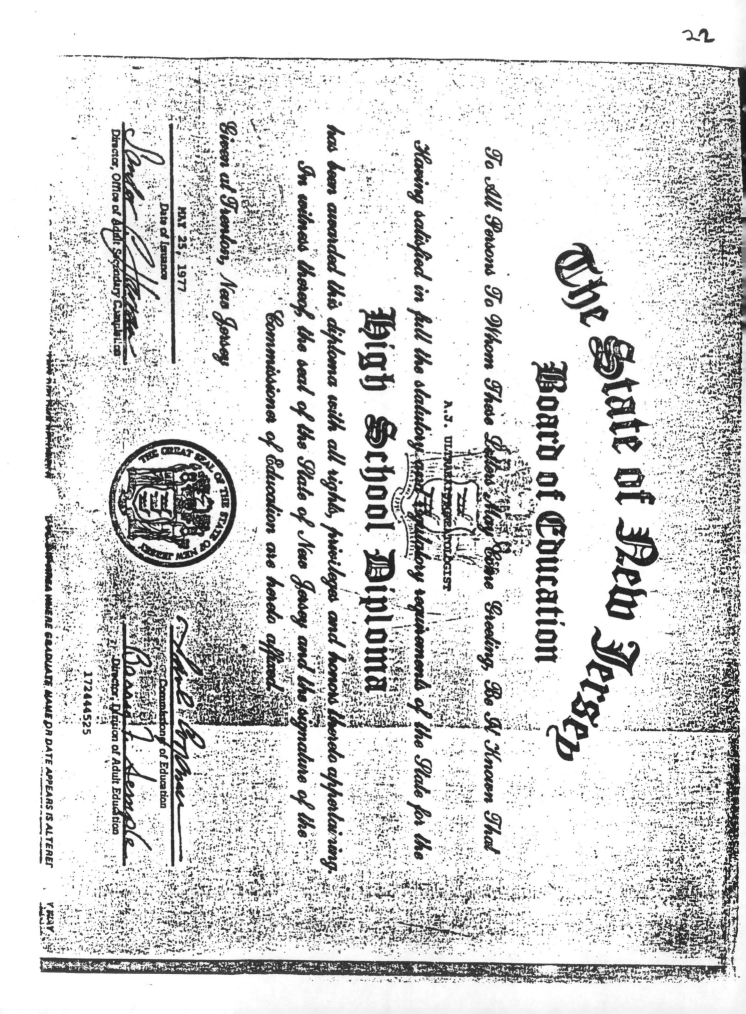

22

The State of New Jersey

Board of Education

To All Persons To Whom These Letters May Come Greeting Be It Known That

N.J. ULTRASTEGE TOLDGIST

Having satisfied in full the statutory and regulatory requirements of the State for the

High School Diploma

has been awarded this diploma with all rights, privileges and honors thereto appertaining.

In witness thereof, the seal of the State of New Jersey and the signature of the

Commissioner of Education are hereto affixed.

Given at Trenton, New Jersey

MAY 25, 1977
Date of Issuance

Director, Office of Adult Secondary Completion

Commissioner of Education

Director, Division of Adult Education

172444525

The State of New Jersey

Board of Education

To All Persons To Whom These Letters May Come Greeting, Be It Known That

Anthony Jesse Williams

Having satisfied in full the statutory and regulatory requirements of the State for the

High School Diploma

has been awarded this diploma with all rights, privileges and honors thereto appertaining.

In witness thereof, the seal of the State of New Jersey and the signature of the

Commissioner of Education are hereto affixed.

Given at Trenton, New Jersey

May 25, 1977
Date of Issuance

Director

Commissioner of Education

1082 46

NJDE 426-14 (Rev. 10/82)

THIS DIPLOMA BECOMES NULL AND VOID IF AREA WHERE GRADUATE NAME OR DATE APPEARS IS ALTERED IN ANY WAY

Universal Life Church, Inc.

Headquarters: 601 - 3rd Street, Modesto, California   (209) 537-0553

This is to certify that + A.J. ULTRAEXISTCREATOLOGIST + — has been awarded a Doctor of Metaphysics Degree this day DECEMBER 1, 1977 by Universal Life Church, Inc., for meritorious recognition upon completion of a course of instruction in the principles of the Universal Life Church.

Doctor of Metaphysics

Kirby J. Hensley
Bishop Kirby J. Hensley, President

Universal Life Church
SEAL
INCORPORATED
MODESTO, CALIFORNIA

Universal Life Church, Inc.

Headquarters: 601 - 3rd Street, Modesto, California   (209) 537-0553

This is to certify that **ANTHONY JESSIE WILLIAMS** has been awarded a Doctor of Metaphysics Degree this day **DECEMBER 1, 19 77** by Universal Life Church, Inc., for meritorious recognition upon completion of a course of instruction in the principles of the Universal Life Church.

Doctor of Metaphysics

SEAL

_____
Bishop Kirby J. HENSLEY, President

26.

Universal Life Church, Inc.

HEADQUARTERS, 601 3RD ST., MODESTO, CALIF. 95351 • (209) 527-0553 OR 527-8111

This is to certify that : ANTHONY J. WILLIAMS •

has been granted the title of : ULTRAEXISTCREATOLOGY

by Universal Life Church, Inc. this day   APRIL 15, 1980

Bishop Brett T. HENSLEY, President

SEAL

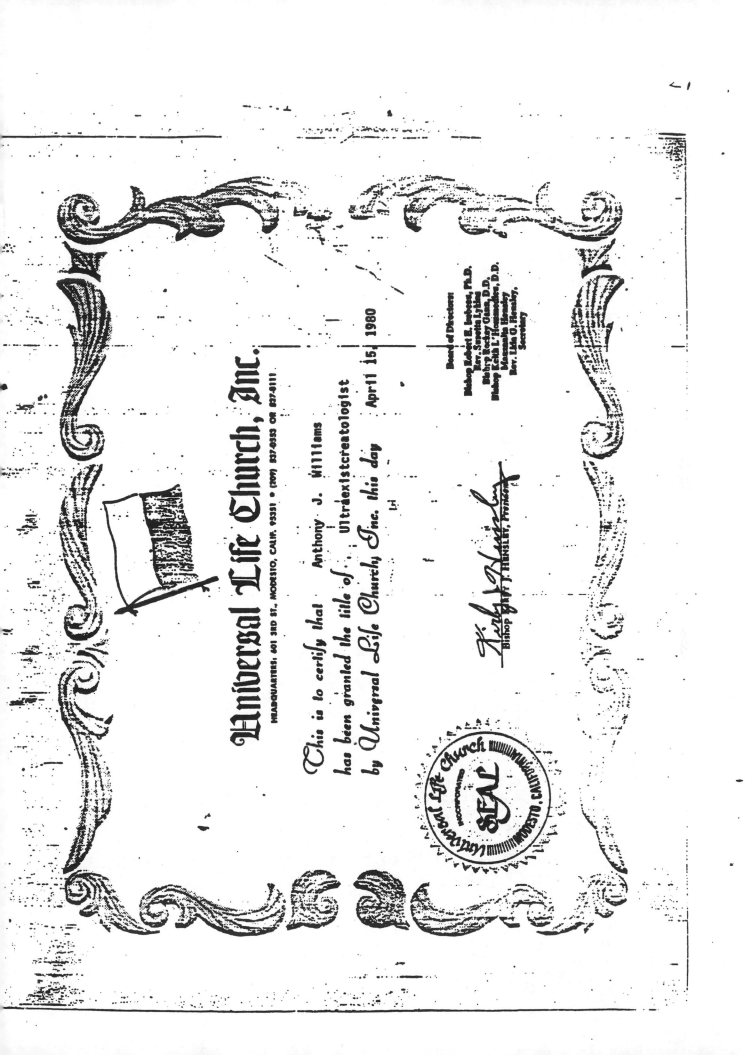

Universal Life Church, Inc.

HEADQUARTERS: 601 3RD ST., MODESTO, CALIF. 95351 • (209) 527-8353 OR 527-9111

This is to certify that Anthony J. Williams

has been granted the title of Ultraexistcreatologist

by Universal Life Church, Inc. this day April 15, 1980

Bishop Kirby J. Hensley, *President*

SEAL — Universal Life Church, INCORPORATED, MODESTO, CALIF.

The Nature of Man of God's Creations

Man became of God only to create and recreate. The
nature of man is this that he and she are only to live life
and to enjoy the infinitive creations of God wherever and
forever God creates, in and out of space and many places.
For we and all life are meaning and meant to live ever last-
ing life, but being over abundant on one planet when we are
meant to go ahead and on to further planets, creations,
spaces and places only cause deaths to decrease the over
population from being stagnant or motionless by the Devil on
one planet. When we are meaning to go on to other planets,
but the Devil keeps us from going in to and on of infinities
of God. Amen. Which means we were never able to be stabil-
ized on one planet when we recognize more than one etcetera.
Amen.

We do know this that there are other life forms which
are similar and non-similar to man and God. The total sum
are of variations such as being inferior, superior, large,
small and tiny. Aslo of a spectrum of colors from one being
to another.

In ultrapolyexistcreatology lives, and non-lives plans
a many destinations, and other than eternity for all kinds
of life, and non-life forms to be, and to live on everlastingly.

Introduction to Ultraexistcreatology

Ultraexistcreatology is an absolute, concise and con-
crete religious educational science which pertains to the
inner and outer beyond existences of creations of God.

Ultraexistcreatology is and are the true and untrue
concepts which deal with space, the universe, life, the beyond, planets and the ultimate of life's existences of
creations of God.

To the nation people will only project a negative attitude of favorable and unfavorable desires and appreciations
on this and these particular subjections and topics.

Societies in general will only begin to attack the
subject and become biased and ignorant to the simplicities
of facts, simply because of this new and old conception.
Which is now the grasp of space, time and nature. The now
focus.

Their criticisms will only allow them our nature not
to understand the view points of which they oppose as facts.

From learning ultraexistcreatology you will understand
that there are other universes, planets and Gods whom are
similar with powers and non-similar to be equivalent with
powers. Many that all cannot or never create to imagine
which are far known in the Ultrapolyexistcreatologies.

Vocabularies Also of an Ultraexistcreatologist

Creatrons, existcreatrons, ultraexistcreatrons, ultra-bioexistcreatrons, and ultrapolyexistcreatrons which mean specific and general electrical fabricated and fabricating elastical functions, circuits and energized impulses of life. Also known as the crystallize Global Satellites and energies of all parts of life involving ultrapolyexist-creatology.

Creatry, existcreatry, ultraexistcreatry, ultrabio-existcreatry and ultrapolyexistcreatry which means the many beyond existences of God's many creations such as the family tree and roots of all life, such as animals, insects, the Solar System, trees, etcetera. The roots of all character-istics of the same family trees of life.

Thesis

The nature of ultraexistcreatology is to explain all phenomena there are in the universe. Observation is one of many keys which emphasizes the esculations of the vast uni-verse also. Meaning man who watches and learns.

The approach is to maintain interest in the field of ultraexistcreatology so that students and teachers will get a better understanding of learning the original aspects attained.

The basic principles of ultraexistcreatology are to reproduce goals, stimulate interest, direction data, prayer, study, achievement and to supply the tools which are needed.

The Introduction of Ultraexistcreatology (Obirthology) means, Universal Christians Religion, Education; Law, Art, Philosophy, Science, Organization, and Theraphy of Obirthologod (God), Amen. Obirtholum-polars; O.B.s also.

Read: Genesis, chapter 1; verse 29

Read: Daniel, chapter 2; verse 11

Read: Dan; chapter 1; verse 12

Read: Ezekiel: chapter 38; verse 20

Read: Genesis; chapter 1; verse 29

These verses are from the Holly Bible, (King James Version)

Also read Genesis: chapter 1; verse 1 (Holly Bible) creatology.

O.B.s schools

Obirtholum-polars:

(Sun/planets)

The Introduction of Ultraexistcreatology (Obirthology) Ultraexistcreatology is the natural prayers and studies of and for life of Obirthologod, amen.

Natural prayers and studies means to follow and obey the universal christians religion, education, law, art, phlosophy, science, organization, and therapy of Obirthologod.

Meaning to consume only the air, water, fruits and vegetables also to obey the natural laws of universe, to help serve creations and other finite creatifications such as man, woman, animals, insects, creatures, organisms, the grass, flowers, bushes and trees etc. throughout the universe as well of God.

Theme

In ultraexistcreatology you will learn that there are
diverse and interchangeable strategies of exploring the old
and the new phenomena there of which are applications and
implications of our given infinitive and expanding universe,
such as to produce facts of the known and unknown which is
the knowledge of the Solar System.

The History of Ultraexistcreatology

From learning ultraexistcreatology you will learn that the history comes, goes, and has always been here since a long time and a long ways. There's no written record yet except this one of ultraxistcreatology.

Ultraexistcreatology is and are the written and non-written laws of proof within the universe. Man at this given time only thinks of the universe as being one Solar System of infinity. Life and we go much further than this. There are much more to learn about ultraexistcreatology the different places of spaces involving more than one universe and Solar System.

The location of ultraexistcreatology is right here and many places everywhere. In this Solar System we live and die within.

Furthermore, references and preferences are our only means of directions and support to travel in other forms of space, but the only problem is this, we never reached the proper inclination or advancement yet of this century. Sufficient supplies was never yet developed to maintain our need and goals satisfactorily.

The History of God and God's Creations

Knowing God is one aspect but knowing the age of our God is another. There is no exact record or age of God and God's creations. God creates infinitively because God beyond existences creates.

There are at most then an infinitive amount of God's creations in creating such as planets, Gods, and the beyond many existences of many creations.

The Relativity and Unrelativity of Ultraexistcreatology

    Ultraexistcreatology relates to various kinds of life
forms whether they are small, large, gigantic or tremendous
in size. Not only this, but many functions which exercise
purpose to associate collectively. Unrelatively life have
or has no meaning when there's no reasoning.

The Transition and Revelation of Ultraexistcreatology

Positively creation is clear to sense when you perceive the logic of the universe. Once the universe centuries ago were peaceful of love, truth and freedom without evil. There was never evil until deliberately the curse of creations became destructions sort of speak the work of the Devil. A negative change which destroys or goes against creations.

The Knowledge and Evidence of Ultraexistcreatology

Ultraexistcreatology is a now, later, and forever science. Only to sense and scope of what is pleasure not violence. To evaluate, manipulate and to probe powerfully when attached to do so. The knowledge is evidence of what exists do creates.

The powers are of God which God given mankind to manipulate and penetrate the beyond existence of God's creations and other than God's creations. God given life thinking capacities to know the meaning of creations. Without God's descriptions of creation mankind will never be living as we are according to God. God given nature the life to exist to create as we are and other than we which are similar from other ultrapolyexistcreatologies.

The History of God and God's Creations

God became of self as of idomeology which means God always exists to create himself or other than this creates and created self. A being which God's existences of many creations became of birth. God also learns from self Godly environments of spaces in ultrapolyexistcreatologies.

They assemble themselves according to what we do here. Their existences of many creations are much more motion and drive within and around flight. The history of God's and Gods' motions are as fast as they want to be. Sometimes they travel as close to the earth and universe or either very far from the earth and the universe. They are unlike us because God creates and created us intentionally this way of birth differently.

Humanity and the Unknown

Man and the unknown simply because a few do not think
as clearly as others, such as difficulties and disabilities,
or either God do or did not intend but for a very few to
know.

This is besides the point; we are all of birth to
recognize this beyond existences of creations within and
built in birth of nature. We do not satisfy or please ourselves according to ultrapolyexistcreatology because we do
not travel to God and other planets.

The Shedding Process of Humanity of Ultraexistcreatology

     · While learning from centuries ago man shed his hairy
or fur protective coat according to the interchange of
nature of God. Man was never without total hair covering
of his or her body. This once was the covering to protect
us from the winter changes of fall. God intended for man
and women to shed only according to spring and summer
weather, but instead God saw fault of the whole entire world
beyond existence of creation. What caused this? The ideals
of destruction and pollution and still centuries later of
God and Man.

The History of Gods and Other than Gods

There are much more to see when evolving here. Not clearly, but such perception can bring you visions if the Gods want or need you to sense them. Being supreme or a supernatural being does not qualify us to be avoided, but yet our only sense can only sense so much. Such as a voice was not yet heard of the Gods. Only mysteriously. They are absolutely similar and non-similar to each other as being Gods of the same family. Such as this philosophy there was once and still is a God who has fell from being because he was kicked out of heaven sort because of doing evil. Now, today and since the beginning it still effects the existence of creation. The God who has fallen from heaven was once an angel.

The Conflict and Irony of Ultraexistcreatology

The reason of conflict and irony because of lack of understanding. No one wants to study ultraexistcreatology but yet only other fields where there are colleges and universities. Ultraexistcreatology is a field all by itself like all courses and fields of study. Ultraexistcreatology is not a perfect science and neither fiction.

There are perfection of other universes, planets, Gods and spaces of ultraexistcreatology that men have not reached physically only thoughtfully; and in addition this is not an exaggeration. Furthermore, there are only different sections of space and many places of spaces in the universe of ultraexistcreatology.

The Public's Opinion About Ultraexistcreatology

Some or most people never even heard of the word, description or pronounciation of ultraexistcreatology, but yet their opinions are pleasing of this sufficient science. They awarded themselves and others of enthusiasm. Their main objections are to learn new and old concepts.

The news media is one problem because people never hear or heard this science being mentioned. T.V. will have a great deal and effect to the public and private camera's eye. View points will be assembled to be shared of one common goal. To listen, speak and see what is happening around us.

The Weakness of Ultraexistcreatology and its Strength

No one is living in perfection but God. We are dying every second but not God. Why is this? The reason is because God and Gods are not like our beyond existence of creation. They are the Gods that are of huge organisms but became most abundant and unlike what we are. We die and we never come back or return to life only mystics allow us to think this way. The weakness is that we are poor and rich but there is no God to save us.

The Student's Role of Learning Ultraexistcreatology

Students will sit and stand to learn the adventures which go about ultraexistcreatology simply because of the advice, routine and attitude this provides them with. Suggestions will be applied and recognized by search and research given for opportunities and employment. If there is enough social interreactions of certainty and concern approaches, and abilities being consistant and provided to further strengthen this particular discipline, synopsis, or symposium, then this will become processed, proclaimed and previsioned.

The Inter-relationships to Understand Nationally and
Internationally of One Another on the Same Planet

How do you or we go about this? As an ultraexistcreatologist we tend to rationalize and be humble with our fellow
men. We need to confirm that there is nothing else to do but
work together rather than having wars with each other.
Simply because we are of the same source but differently
creating and created by God. The reason why there and here
are ammunition, artillery, military and weapons because we
are all frightened and petrified of the opened and closed
infinitive spaces of time and the universe. Being afraid
caused an artificial and negative force field which generated
our planet of being and destroying every life form because
of misinterpretation against one another and around each
other. The reason why it became this type of danger and
destruction also because of the Gods interferences of no
transitions and no absolute positive wave patterns coming or
transmitting in the heavens. This is one of the reasons
why criminal conducts are still effecting our planet from
the past, present and future. As a religious educational
scientist, I believe today that true love is just a waste
of time according to the Devil or Devils in and outside of
space. There is no help to be saved until God and our planet
and others of the known and unknown planets throughout

ultrapolyexistcreatology work and play together. Succeeding
this that we all work and enjoy each other.

The Female Mother of the Begining of Time of *ultraexistcreatology* (OB)

The Female Mother of the begining of time bear two opposite equally sexual offsprings. The two opposite equally sexual offsprings fed off their mother's breast (mammory glands) the male baby (infant) fed off the mother's strong side/the female infant fed on her mother's weak side at birth.

This once was the mother's births in transition of the two opposite equally sexual offsprings of Obirthologod. Amen

Furthermore, the many opposite equally sexual offsprings bear also, but many finite numbers strong side baby males, weak side females (babies) lava, eggs, cafes, cats, dogs, rabbits, insects, plants of that nature bear either two or many opposite equally sexual offsprings of Obirthologods. Amen

Two opposite equally sexual offsprings each in the begining of time. Those whom bear forth two opposite equally sexual offsprings and from two opposite equally sexual offsprings that bear many opposite equally sexual offsprings as well but of two types of offsprings differently of Obirthologod. Amen

The Devish God's Judgements

Which marks upon the Ultraexistcreatologists the testimony of once was nature now un-natural nature of Devilish God's. The Devilish God's influence, cause us and nature to attack and accurse us mentally, individually, accurse verbally, physically, socially, environmentally, and universally.

Furthermore, to misjudge, judge positive, neutrally, and negatively of an unballanced nature. Amen

Also, in the beginning, their were two opposite equally sexual offsprings, and the two opposite equally sexually offsprings they bring forth many opposite equally sexually offsprings in finite numbers of Obirthologod's. Amen

The entire Solar System were air, water, fruits, vegetarians, according to our nature and other life forms like ourselves of Obirthologod's. Amen

The Answers and Questions of Ultraexistcreatology

What is ultraexistcreatology? Ultraexistcreatology is
a religious educational science dealing with the universal
life of God.

Who is ultraexistcreatology? All life forms throughout
the universe. When was ultraexistcreatology started? Since
life became the very first of many. Only our ancestors know
and have known how God created them. Only God knows which
is kept concealed from us.

There are many more answers and questions than these.
This is to just give an example of how enthusiasms digest
and perceive.

The Wars of the Gods and the Attacking of Our Planet

As I say and have said before, it is the deception of a God and Gods like a Devil or Devils against their own nature and ours. Under the evil powers of God and the Devil only brings down confusions and an unbalance of the Gods' nature and throughout ours. We cannot control this emotion nor function, and neither can we avoid this penalty. They have such powers only to do evil and eventually they will destroy themselves if they are not careful, but their demands are to only destroy our natural resources instead of theirs. The problem is this that we are all endangered and we cannot get or fly out of this whole, and we cannot get rid of the Devil neither the devilish God or Gods. They are only tampering with our universe and others.

The Wars Between Other Planets and Locations in Spaces

What can you do or them in many situations as violence up, below, and around the infinitive spacious universe? Nothing, but be destroyed and die. Man in general thinks there is no such thing happening. Why? Because he does not sense the exact torments happening; but, yet to his planet and because man does not have enough insight to recognize this disposal happening. God creates and exists to create fragile and substantial in and around the universe, but destruction falls from the mind being of the super-natural or supreme being sort of speak.

The Traveling of Man Who Walks in the Sun
of Ultraxistcreatology

The Sun's rays and penetrations give and provide man
with being colored or darkened by heat of the rotating sun.
Man centuries ago also centered himself in the sun. Man
walked and rode animals of all kinds such as elephants,
horses, camels, gigantic dinosaurs and birds in the Sun.
This is one of the reasons why we have all kinds of darken
complexions such as yellow, orange, red, brown and black
because of the sun. Before shedding hair man had a complex-
ion of being white, but when shedding men and women began to
change darken complexions, and still, since centuries ago,
the colorations continue to effect and color us from one
shade to another. When our original complexions were just
having hairy fur coats and under our coats just white, pink
and slightly yellow skin. The sun also can and could penetrate through our fur coats, and our shedding fur coats.
Our protective layer of hair.

The Diagram and Illustrations of God, Gods, Devil
and the Devils Interreactions, Non
Interreactions and Affiliations

God Himself

Gods Themselves

God vs God

God vs Gods   Positive Powers

Gods vs God

Gods vs Gods

Devil Himself

Devils Themselves

Devil vs Devil

Devil vs Devils

Devils vs Devil   Negative Powers

Devils vs Devils

God Himself vs Devil Himself

Gods Themselves vs Devils Themselves

God vs Devil

Devil vs God

Gods vs Devil   Positive & Negative Powers

Devils vs Gods

Devil Himself vs God Himself

Devils Themselves vs Gods Themselves

Devil vs God

God vs Devil

Devils vs God   Negative & Positive Powers

Gods vs Devils

Devil Himself vs Devil Himself

Devils Themselves vs Devils Themselves

Devil vs Devil

Devil vs Devils

Devils vs Devil   Negative vs Negative Powers

Devils vs Devils

Reaction

The American Federal Government is not assisting this course of science. And there are no fundings to help this program, neither no institutions who recommend this to be acknowledged of this and these types of philosophies and concepts. A poor scientist, a rich institution.

O I say O come O I forvegetables (air, water, Fruits, /vegetables) of oBirtholoGod / (air, water, Fruits, /vegetables) of oBirtholoGods names, powers/ Glories o I say o come Hapcebiousrep-th-meets. Amen. O come Hap cebious rep ta meets: meaning, oBirtholoGod / oBirtholoGods. Amen. Universal Christians R.E.L.A.P.-S.O.- Therapy of oBirtholoGod / oBirtholoGods. Amen. Sunday 13th. Ultraexistcreatologists also. Amen.

COMMONWEALTH OF PENNSYLVANIA · DEPARTMENT OF HEALTH
VITAL RECORDS

Certification of Birth

DATE OF BIRTH: 12-08-54
(MO. DAY. YEAR)

FILE NO.: 2416280-54

DATE FILED: 01-11-55
(MO. DAY. YEAR)

COUNTY OF BIRTH: PHILADELPHIA

DATE ISSUED: 04/04/90
(MO. DAY. YEAR)

SUBJECT: A. J. ULTRAEXISTCREATOLOGIST

SEX: MALE

This is to certify that this is a true copy of the record which is on file in the Pennsylvania Department of Health, in accordance with Act 66 P.L. 304, approved by the General Assembly, June 29, 1953.

Charles Hardester

CHARLES HARDESTER
STATE REGISTRAR

H105.105 (REV 8-1-86)

COMMONWEALTH OF PENNSYLVANIA
★ DEPARTMENT OF HEALTH ★

4879705

SOCIAL SECURITY: 172-44-4525 DATE: 09/27/88 Major: Human Services/Case Aide

NAME: Mr. Anthony J Ultraexistcreato
ADDRESS: 306 Cooper Street
Camden   NJ 08102

PHONE: 609-541-0578

TRANSCRIPT — PAGE # 1

COURSE NUMBER	COURSE DESCRIPTION	GRADE	ATTEMPTED CREDITS	EARNED CREDITS
******	Fall 1973	*****	*****	*****
80-040	Basic Reading Skill II	C	2.00	2.00
	Term GPA = 2.000/Term Credits =>		2.00	2.00
******	Spring 1974	*****	*****	*****
80-260	English Comp I	C	3.00	3.00
80-010	Introduction Human Services	B	3.00	3.00
80-010	Basic Psychology	C	3.00	3.00
80-010	Introduction To Sociology	C	3.00	3.00
	Term GPA = 2.250/Term Credits =>		12.00	12.00
******	Spring 1975	*****	*****	*****
80-200	Biology I-Science	C	3.00	3.00
80-270	English Comp II	F	3.00	3.00
80-140	Minority History II	B	3.00	3.00
J-030	Introduction To College Math I	C	3.00	3.00
	Term GPA = 1.666/Term Credits =>		9.00	6.00
******	Summer 1975	*****	*****	*****
80-100	Intermediate Algebra	W		
80-020	Psych-Personality/Adjustment	C	3.00	3.00
	Term GPA = 2.000/Term Credits =>		3.00	3.00
******	Fall 1975	*****	*****	*****
80-250	Man & Environment	B	3.00	3.00
80-060	Introduction To Counseling	B	3.00	3.00
80-030	American Federal Government	F	3.00	3.00
80-070	Social Psychology	B	3.00	3.00
80-050	Criminology	C	3.00	3.00
	Term GPA = 2.000/Term Credits =>		15.00	12.00
******	Spring 1976	*****	*****	*****
80-100	Contemporary Health Studies	B	1.00	1.00
80-130	Minority History	B	3.00	3.00
80-020	Social Work Processes	F		
80-050	Child Psychology	F		
80-020	Social Problems	F		
	Term GPA = 1.714/Term Credits =>		7.00	4.00

COURSE NUMBER	COURSE DESCRIPTION	GRADE	ATTEMPTED CREDITS	EARNED CREDITS
******	Fall 1978	*****	*****	*****
070-240	Human Biology	W		
520-100	Intermediate Algebra	W		
760-050	Child Psychology	W		
760-070	Social Psychology	W		
	Term GPA = 0.000/Term Credits =>		0.00	0.0
******	Spring 1979	*****	*****	*****
070-240	Human Biology	W		
400-140	Minority History II	W		
430-020	Social Work Processes	W		
520-020	Basic Math Skills II-Elem Alg	W		
	Term GPA = 0.000/Term Credits =>		0.00	0.0

	GRADUATION CREDITS	EARNED CREDITS	ATTEMPTED CREDITS	QUALITY POINTS	GRADE AVERAGE
• CUMULATIVE TOTALS	34.00	34.00	43.00	81.0	1.88

• CUMULATIVE TOTALS INCLUDE ONLY DEGREE CREDIT COURSES.

REGISTRAR

Mr. Anthony J Ultraexistcreato
306 Cooper Street
Camden   NJ 08102

STATE OF NEW JERSEY
DEPARTMENT OF EDUCATION
3535 QUAKERBRIDGE ROAD
CN 503
TRENTON, N.J. 08625-0503

DIVISION OF ADULT EDUCATION

SAUL COOPERMAN, COMMISSIONER

March 20, 1989

A.J. Ultraexistcreatologist
Holly B
Ancora Psychiatric Hospital
P.O.-Hammonton, New Jersey 08037

To whom it may concern:

This will confirm that a New Jersey State High School Diploma was awarded to the person named below under Option II of a set of high school graduation options available to adults in New Jersey. An award of a state high school diploma under Option II is made after evaluation of a candidate's college transcript. A person must have met minimum state requirements which were in force on the date the diploma was awarded.

Name of graduate: A.J. Ultraexistcreatologist
Social security number: 172-44-4525
Date diploma awarded: May 25, 1977

Sincerely yours,

Sandor Hayman
Manager,
Office of Administration
  and Management Services

SH/LB26

A representation of the ultrapolyexistcreatologies:
such as the beyond all true infinitive many existences of
God's many Creations etcetera. Amen. Meaning such as space,
spaces, Idomiology, universe, universes, and planets (obirtholumpolars) etcetera. A diagram below of various complexions
emphasized of the ultrapolyexistcreatologies:

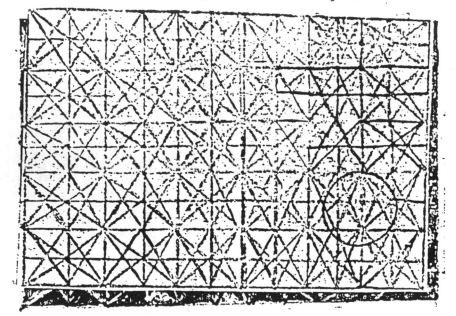

Courtesy of the ultraexistcreatologist and the church and
college of ultraexistcreatology and ultrapolyexistcreatology
Anthony J. Williams.

Ultraexistcreatology

Ultraexistcreatology discribes the differences in meaning and powers-indestructible powers of each word in meaning from the heaven, the Ultrapolyexistcreatologies. Amen

Idomeology	Idomiology
Obirthologod	Obirthologods
Sun	Moon (Obirthology)
Man	Woman
Male-baby	Female-baby
Male-babies	Female-babies

Ultrapolyexistcreatologies, Ultrabioexistcreatologies; Finite numbers of humans, insects, animals, plants and trees in creatifications.

The Formulation of What Idomeology Means

Idomiology means: Also pertains to Ultrabioexistcreatology of the Ultrapoly-existcreatology. Amen

Idomeclogy	Idomiology
Obirthologod	Obirthologods
Sun	Moon (obirthology)
Man	Woman
Male	Female

The History of Devilish Gods. Amen.

Amen: Means to be blessed or blessings, to be free without evils, various creatifications.

The Develish Gods have no ruler over them, but yet they were created by their family trees to be also and to live indestructibly like their very powerful and creative Devilish Godly families. Amen

Devilish Gods creates all kinds of violences, accidents, misterious acts, numbers, and judgements and especially also un-natural creatifications deliberately. Furthermore, makes false accusations. Amen.

The judgements against us over family shall never be avoided until the end of time-creation.

Also, what I like to speak/write about: after/before creations/universes. These universes before us also were destroyed and a few not many or/ and very many are still living or has been dead. Amen

Creation Learning by Man from Obirthologod.   Amen

The natural and un-natural creation that man, woman, animals, insects creatures, plants/trees learn/change from of God. Amen

First of all, what is natural creation? Natural creation is pure creation without defects and consuming air, water, fruits/vegetables living in the enviroment and worshiping Obirthologods.   Amen

Un-natural creations are man made things learning also of Devilish Gods/ and disobeying the Universal Christians R.E.-L.A.P.-S.O.-Therapy of Obirthologod(s).   Amen

Natural creations are forever being in creation, if so, indestructible by Obirthologods. Amen

From the Intro-to Ultraexistcreatologys may Obirthologod(s) provide you with such an insight to understand the various concepts, structures, behaviors, contours, measures, powers, and distributions of innerspace as well as being of outer space as well. Thankyou.

Prof: Rev, Dr. A.J. Ultraexistcreatologist

Now the Sun runs from the tn (OBirthology/9ies)
- moon the now focus more until the eclipse
is mee (then total destruction). Amen.

This is the Graduation Ceremony for those students who have attained the requirements of becoming Ultraexistcreatologists.

First of all, I will love to thank you for your achievements, and concerns in helping this course and organization gain status, recognition, and purpose of this typical and particular (R.E.L.A.P.S.O.) Religion, Education, Law, Art, Philosophy, Science, Organization.

Also, I will love to say - Keep up the excellent work, research, rank, assurance, potential, business, and prosperity of this course of Ultraexistcreatology and Ultraexistcreatologies.

My respect for you as a Student Class Graduate Government are my appreciatio logics, goals, success, practice, and profession of God who created this Religion Education, Law, Art, Philosophy, Science, organization for you and I to learn gloriously of one another and God.

Also to teach one another of your old and new Religious educational, law, art, philosophical, scientific, and organizational experiences, concepts, predictions, prayer, study, enjoyment and creativities of and with God. Amen.

As you shall acknowledge this universal School of Thought which is only accredited and enriched of Ocomehapcebiousreptameets and Obsreptameets meaning O I Say O come O I Lovegetables O I Say O come Holy Altra polycreatexistbirthology religion, education, preacher, teacher, association, meets, and R.E.L.A.P.S.O.. meaning, Religion, Education, Law, Art, Philosophy, as well as Science and organization of the Ultrapolyexistcreatologies, God, etcetera. Amen.

Ocomehapcebiousreptameets and obsreptameets meaning, O I Say O come o

I Lovegetables O I Say O come Holy Altra poly createxistbirthology,

religion, education, preacher, teacher, association, meets, and R.E.L.A.P.S.C

meaning Religion, Education, Law, Art, Philosophy, as well as Science and

organization of the Ultrapolyexistcreatologies, God, etcetera. Amen.

Note: An Ultraexistcreatologist or Ultrapolyexistcreatologists means

 to sense the purification of divine love for God and God's creations,

etcetera. Amen.

    To have you as a class apart of the student class graduate govern-

ment (creation of God) is only to greet, meet, and inform you of what

you were unconscientiously   acknowledging the Introduction of Ultra-

existcreatology, until after you realized this phenomena. Amen.

    Thank you for your attention and support of being here.

                              Sincerely yours,

                              A.J. Ultraexistcreatologist

                              Ultraexistcreatologist

                              A.J. Ultraexistcreatologist

NOTE: Ultraexistcreatology also means finite and infinitive existence

of God's creations and other than God's finite and infinitive

existence of creation. Amen.

This is an after and before entry examination of an Ultraexistcreatological Questionnaire and Test for the people of non-denominational thought and non-traditional doctrine, but to only acknowledge or to believe of what is absolutely proof and right of knowledge and power of God; and to recognize what God is saying, meaning, and creating of all of what the universes, planets, spaces, Ultrapolyexistcreatologies, infinities, finities, animals, insects, creatures, trees, air, water, mountains, ecetera, of God. Amen.

What does the power consist of what God can or shall do?

Describe the power of what God is or is made of. What is the experience of Ultraexistcreatology? Explain.

Do you believe in Ultraexistcreatology? What are the powers of God?

Why do you believe in Ultraexistcreatology?

What is Ultraexistcreatology? Do you confess your sins of or to people, God, etcetera?

Where did Ultraexistcreatology come from or of? Why does the Devil take or move your or our souls? Why does the Devil enter our souls? Why are there Ultrapolyexistcreatologies? What do you believe? Why do you believe in what you believe?

Where is God?

Why do you want to take the course of Ultraexistcreatology?

Why is God being God?

Who created us?

Do you accept Ultraexistcreatology as a prayer and a study of God?

Why God created us and others then us? What is the purpose of you to be or not to be of Ultraexistcreatology? What is the purpose of Ultraexistcreatology? Does Ultraexistcreatology mean life, mind, power, soul, spirit and body? What is the purpose and ritual of God and God's creations? Describe, please.

Do you believe in Jesus Christ and God? Why are we here? Will or shall you devote your life and time to Ultraexistcreatology? Do you believe in Moses and God? Do you believe in God?

Does Ultraexistcreatology relate to other sciences, philosophies, religions, educations, sports, laws and arts of God? Explain.

Who is the founder of Ultraexistcreatology? God or man, etcetera? Please explain. What are the six definitions and concepts of the hand?

Is God the creator of Ultraexistcreatology?

Is Life the creator of Ultraexistcreatology?

Who is the original creator or founder of Ultraexistcreatology and the Ultrapolyexistcreatology? Please explain.

God and Man. What is the purpose of man, God, the universe, planets, infinity and space?

What does the universe consist of?

What is the meaning of Idomeology and Idomiology?

What is the definition of o come Hapcebiousreptameets?   Please
explain in long terms.

What does Universal christians Religion,
Education, law, Art, Philosophy, Science, organization,
therapy of oBirtholoGod/ oBirtholoGods also. Amen.,
means? (Air, Water, Fruits, Vegetables) and
those supreme Beings are also indestructible
and of Indestructabilities/foreverlasting(s).
throughout those/these ultra poly existreatologies,
(oBirtthologies), Idomiologies/Idomeologies also. Amen
what are the OBs. Schools, Systems, Golden Rules
also? please explain in long terms/exactly
what they are/to be continuously? Amen.
why do all learn from/of one another also
as well of OBirtholoGod (s) also? Amen.
why does not Knowledge never ends Also? Amen.

Better/Worse Judgements of Devilish Gods. Amen

Devilish Gods makes us lie, cheat, steal/kill; makes us eat food (deathologies such as of other animals; and animals eat each other and attack one another.

Devilish Gods are for the worse/better such as in an un-natural universe we think its natural or one or many thinks or know they are better than one another. O if you are real tall/strong the other person may not be, causes jeolousy etc.

The worse of Devilish Gods are to judge wrong/control us to do wrong as they tamper with the universe. Better Judgements are being vegetarians.

Synopsis: Of The Introduction of Ultraexistcreatology (Obirthology)

Ultraexistcreatology explains various emphasizes and has various concepts and meanings about creations in which man/woman knows and don't know.

The creatifications of Idomeology/idomiology are different in meaning. Idomeology means: God has always been here until God creates self and created others etc. Amen. Idomiology means: God creates/created others etcetera and there are others besides God himself in which God has not created also visavis etc. Amen.

Also about the first of creation man/woman are to bring forth their opposite equally sexual offsprings on the mother's strong side, male baby, and on her weak side female baby of obirthologod.

Since the beginning man/woman, and all life were once consuming the air, water, fruits and vegetables according to ultraexistcreatologists of obirthologod. Amen. Also man/woman walked as circling (rotated, walked around the large earth) as the land was inbetween north/south waters (the oceans), but God has moved (detroyed) the land as it circled the globe. Language began to change into many and people also became un-natural after what they saw the earth, people, and life done of God.

From the winds of the destruction certain by they the first created and after us knew we became illogical/un-natural. From that also criminals became of a devilish God.

Ultraexistcreatology is to learn about such past is to provide for a successful future to maintain natural resources and to listen to what obirthologod says to you U.C.R.E.-L.A.P.-S.O.-therapeutically (Jesus Christ). Amen.

October 31, 1984

Dear President of the United States of America:

May you acknowledge this new science along with your fellow men.

May you please share this contribution with all people you know and don't know.

The reason why I am writing you is because life is very difficult to get a publisher to publish this material or even to get the manuscript on the news or TV.

That is why I contribute it to you and address it also to the nation.

May God bless you and keep you in perfect health to do your duty, because you are a beauty when you are in the right of God. Amen.

When you receive this contribution, read it, and after you read it, then write me on how you feel about my contribution of appreciation of God. Amen.

I am going to write a prayer for you and your family and the nation.

Dear God May you bless and help the president of the United States and the United States as well as other nations to do perfect where ever you, I or we go to live. May you see that all of us are only humans but unlike your beyond existence of creation God to live a successful life.

May you see that all never harm each other or curse God, and may you bless all, because we all are inferior to you God, because of our love of another level of beings

within the ultrapolyexistcreatologies. Amen.

Sincerely yours, *Anthony J. Williams*

Rev. Dr. Anthony J. Williams
Ultraexistcreatologist
Northgate II
Apt. #701
500 N. 7th Street
Camden, NJ 08102
609-365-4890 or 609-662-1997

GOD'S BOOK OF KNOWLEDGE

The Godly Book - The Book of God for Life's Comprehension of the heavenly bodies, etcetera. Learn the R.E.L.A.P.S. of Ultraexistcreatology. Ultraexistcreatology is actually the Religion, Education, Law, Art, Philosophy and Science of God. Meaning to pray, and study the R.E.L.A.P.S. of Ultrapolyexistcreatology and God. Amen.

This is one of many purposes of God. Amen.

God is glorious of purification.

God is glorious of himself.

God is glorious of power. God is glorious of being indestructible to himself.

God is glorious of infinity. God is glorious of being near or far to himself.

God is glorious of creation. God is glorious of being visible or invisible to himself, and towards others.

God is glorious of peace. God is glorious of being finite.

God is glorious of love. God is glorious of feelings.

God is glorious of truth. God is glorious of being sensitive.

God is glorious of freedom. God is glorious of being fast or slow to himself. God is glorious of the Ultrapolyexistcreatology.

God is glorious of being without evil. Amen.

This is the true soul and spirit of God's being the inside, outside, and surroundings, of God himself.

By

A.J. Ultraexistcreatologist

The Introduction of Ultraexistcreatology (Obirthology) means, Universal Christians Religion, Education, Law, Art, Philosophy, Science, Organization, and Therapy of Obirthologod (God). amen. Obirtholum-polars; C.B.s. also.

Read the following chapters from the Holly Bible (King James Version;

Daniel, chapter 2, verse 11

Daniel , chapter 1 verse 12

Ezekiel, chapter 38, verse 20

Genesis, chapter 1, verse 29

Genesis, chapter 1, verse 1 (Holly Bible) creatology.

O.B.s schools, Obirtholum-polars: (Sun/planets)

The Introduction of Ultraexistcreatology (Obirthology)

The adult female mother (birthcreator) are to bear bring fourth two **opposite** equally sexual offsprings; on her week side baby female offspring; and on her strong side male baby offspring of obirthology of Obirthologod. amen.

And of the two opposite equally sexual offsprings are the many opposite equally sexual offsprings such as different types of species whom bear two opposite equally sexual offsprings or many (types) opposites equallly sexual offsprings centuries ago of Obirthologod. amen. Obirtholum-polars (Sun/planets)

By Professor: A.J. Ultraexistcreatologist

The Religion of Ultraexistcreatology

The Religion of Ultraexistcreatology is the prayer of God's love and our love for Creation.

To communicate religiously without evil thoughts and doings of the Devil.

The religion of Ultraexistcreatology is the ritual of God.

The religion and ritual of God is to love and be loved of all creations rather than total destructions.

The Education of Ultraexistcreatology is to accredit, enrich, appreciate, study, unify, explore, sense, explain, penetrate and inform all of what you experience of God and God's creations. Also, to supply tests for the enthused student or class of people who are interested in learning the intrinsic, and extrinsic powers of God, whether of the mind, perception of God, body, environment, space, the universe, planets, finites, infinities, pronounciation of God's vocabulary, the concepts of God's and man's creativities, etcetera. Amen.

Furthermore, to speculate of association positively of God. Amen.

The Law of Ultraexistcreatology

Ultraexistcreatology controls and uncontrols nature of God.

The law of ultraexistcreatology is to love and belove of our natural creations as well as God and what ever God creates regardless of what authority they may have or creates. The second law is to do not deny or create negatively within or around God or God's creations and other then God's creations. Also means, to enforce tolerance, attention, regulation, rules, roles, and control of the universe. The third is to enjoy all what ever exist to create (existcreatology) or beyond exist to create (ultraexistcreatology). Which is the and of the ultrapolyexistcreatologies. The ultrapolyexist-creatological law or universal law of God which means our life lives and dies and after death we go into another form or no form at all of the ultrapolyexistcreatological being. Note: Death means, we go back where and when God first created or creates life to return where life such as us first with out form and life began. The theory of an ultraexist-creatologist only means various levels and detections in creations of facts and experiences of God, but only remains untrue or not proven to others of the Devil or just of a negative and positive change of what is not acknowledged clearly.

An example of ultrabioexistcreatology.

First of all ultrabioexistcreatology means prayer and
study of the beyond two existences of God's two creations.
Such as the opposites of what God creates or not opposites
at all of what you acknowledge here of creation.

Day and night	Life and death
Air and water	Life and life after death
Male and female	Appearance/vanishing points
Infant and adult	Apearing/disappearing
God and Devil	Logics/Illogics
Large and small	
Solid and soft	
Sweet and sour	
Wet and dry	
Hot and cold	
After and Before creatifications	

Female: In the beginning of Gods (OBirthoria)
creations are to birth two opposites (sexes);each (1m + 1F)
(male/female) equally but of different genders(offsprings
of OBirth ology god. amen.

Idomeology: (sun, male and strong) also God;
Idomiology (OBirthology, moon, female and weak)
of OBirthology god. amen. We were giants as tall as that

Adam /Eve: The first created (man/woman)
of OBirthology god. Amen. The Sun / planets (OBirtholom-
during the beginning light up the entire universe, abled longa
was

The Art of Ultraexistcreatology

The art of Ultraexistcreatology is the creative acting, gymnastics, dance, song, art, poetry (poetologist), philosophy, living conditions, prayer, study, and an enrichment of experience of God and Creation.

Furthermore, Ultraexistcreatology is a religious educational scientific art of God.

In order to maintain this type of perception, we must accept this type of life of God and other than God's creation as long as there is peace, love, truth, and freedom without violence.

The Philosophy of Ultraexistcreatology

The philosophy of ultraexistcreatology is the prayer, study, enrichment, appreciation, communication, to love gloriously of God and God's creations and other than God's creations. To express verbally and thoughtfully of all acknowledgements of the Ultrapolyexist-creatologies. Amen.

NOTE: God does consist of Ultrapolyexistcreatrons and obsreptameetrons, meaning infinitive powers of Ocomehapcebiousreptameets (ocome have happened and been sent by all of us - religion, education, preacher, teacher, association, meets - also God.

Furthermore, an ultraexistcreatologist or ultrapolyexistcreatologists are the profession and conviction of the Religious, Educations, Laws, Arts, Philosophies, Sciences of God, etcetera. Amen.

NOTE: You are an Ultraexistcreatologist and Ultrapolyexistcreatologists by (birth) the nature of God. Amen.

To be Ultraexistcreatologists or not to be Ultrapolyexistcreatologists of God. Amen.

Also in Ultraexistcreatology means, the mind, body, soul, spirit, environment, space, God, the planets, the universe, infinities, heavenly spiritual bodies, etcetera. Amen.

The Art of Ultraexistcreatology

The art of Ultraexistcreatology is the actual performance
of being positive, dance, song, talk, art, communication,
gymnastics, poetry, (poetologist), prayer, study, enjoyment
of God, etcetera.

The Philosophy of Ultraexistcreatology

The philosophy of Ultraexistcreatology is to guide positive
speech - accurately and constructively of speculation, search
and research deligently of God.

THE SCIENCE OF ULTRAEXISTCREATOLOGY

The Science of Ultraexistcreatology is the history, prediction, paradigms, forces, signs, God, the Universe, Sense of Perception, and logic around infinity of the Ultrapolyexistcreatologies. Also in ultraexistcreatology means GOD can and shall create GOD himself any creation desire of himself. Regardless of what type of appearance, size or creation GOD is, or whatever of such all true (altra or ultra) infinitive everlasting powers, characteristics, logics, knowledge and perceptions ever created and creating of the ultrapolyexistcreatological life of GOD. AMEN.

The Organization of Ultraexistcreatology

The organization is the foundation and recognition of God and God's Creations. Such as Creations are to live perfect within and around God and the creation of God without destruction. Meaning, mentally, physically, socially, environmentally, and universally to live without evils of God in God's creations.   Amen.

The organization of Ultraexistcreatology is the fundamentals of conformity, encouragement, pleasure, love, facts, reception, administration exchange, importance, dignity, and explorations of all contours of God.   Amen.

THE THERAPY OF ULTRAEXISTCREATOLOGY.

This particular therapy is to have everyone acknowledge GOD, etcetra. Everyone does not think the same as of what GOD may look like or to be of what GOD is actually to others, because GOD sees in them as we sense the difference of what GOD may be.

Everyone has a sense of intelligence to describe what GOD may be doing or what is GOD like of the high heavens.

GOD informs everyone of GOD's powerful creations and variations of GOD himself. This is why we have and give various informations and revelations of what GOD may be at that time, but creates finite or infinitely of GOD himself and of other creations as what we may sense of an open mind (conscientiousness). We are to help one another to serve the GOD we know of and became of in creation.

Furthermore, as an Ultraexistcreatologist to carry on Religion, Education, Law, Art, Philosophy, Science and organization of what Ultraexistcreatologists can and shall do. Such as to apply many positive outlooks on search and research prayer, study, comparative prayers, studies and enjoyments of and around God.

No one knows when GOD may save the Ultrapolyexistcreatologies, but GOD himself is the only one who may know.

NOTE: The Idomeological and Idomiological GOD and GODS I recognized are of various aspects such as positive, neutra, and negative, etcetra. Also, there are many other creations other than GOD's which are positive, neutra, and negative, etcetra, of the Ultrapolyexistcreatologies and Ultrapolyexistcreatry, and Ultrapolyexistcreatrons, but unlike GOD, GODS, Devil, Devils and many other destructions and creations in or of the Ultrapolyexistcreatologies. AMEN.

By A. J. Ultraexistcreatologist

GOD has various names according to various languages of the Ultrapolyexistcreatologies.   AMEN.

Appreciate loving but there and here is no guarantee you will be loved in these days of time because the Devil and Devils are destroying us Ultrapolyexistcreatologically speaking and writing live and let us be live of GOD, all creations, because destruction will only be and shall be destroyed of the Ultrapolyexistcreatrons and antiultrapolyexistcreatrons.   AMEN.

NOTE: Ultrapolyexistcreatologizes means powers, speed, and energy of GOD
        and other than of then GOD's creation fast or slow speed, etcetera.

NOTE:

To inform of what you acknowledge and acknowledged what others may explain, or acknowledge and experienced.

POSTSCRIPT:

This is the Religious Educational Lawful Artful Philosophical Scientific organization about the Ultrapolyexistcreatologies and GOD.   AMEN.

THE SUPERIOR AND SUPREME (Ultrapolyexistcreatological school or schools of Religion, Education, Law, Art, Philosophy, Science organization of GOD etcetera. AMEN.

What cause GOD to separate creations such as creating different types of planets (Obirtholumpolars) and other creativities such as finite and infinite creations rather than to be all together of one another of the same and whole entire Ultrapolyexistcreatologies (abundantly all together rather than to be of separations of various creations? To be together rather than divided.

The reason why because GOD remains to be jealous and forced by Satan to cause anticreations (anticreatologies) such as not to be of love of our entire Ultrapolyexistcreatologies.

Also cause our particular planet to be destroyed by one another throughout outer space (Ultraexistcreatologies) and inner space as well. This is one of the main reasons, revelations and effects of our given true reality that we all are not enjoying one another because we are not all together as one infinite family such as our families of the variations of the Ultrapolyexistcreatologies are not all together as a whole as one long perfect extreme, platform or plain.

Yes, as I sense GOD telling me this, that our main observation is that GOD also sees and has seen fault of what GOD does, did and has done to his (GOD's) and our creations.

Furthermore, GOD said GOD shall recreate, and create but the Devil will and shall destroy our creation and others. Amen.

NOTE:

We all are separated such as the planets of our families and other creations but we acknowledge them that we do all beyond exist to create of GOD, GODS, and Ultrapolyexistcreatologies. Amen

The Therapy of Ultraexistcreatology is to be positive, realistic, honest, perfect, to be of love, peace, truth, and freedom for all without evils, etcetera. Amen.

Also to enforce cermonial prayers of religion of the field of Ultraexistcreatology and study (Education) to harvest the plantation and speak with GOD etcetera. Amen.

U.C.R.E.L.A.P.S.O. Therapy of Obirthologod and Obirthologods:
Acknowledge praises to the GOD the Ultrapolyexistcreatrons and obsreptameetrons.
NOTE: Religion, Education, Law, Art, Philosophy, Science, and organization is our discipline, prayer, Study, Righteousness, Creation, Communication, Intelligence and positive attribution of GOD. Amen. (Ultrapolyexistcreatrons) means after, before, and so on, simultaneously been here, eternity, forever, etcetera.

O I Say O Come O I Lovegetables, O I Say O Come Hapcebious Rep-Ta-Meets;
O I Say O Come O I Lovegetables, O I Say O Come Have Happen and been sent by all
of U.S.R.E.P.T.A. meets O I Say O Come O I Lovegetables O I Say O Come Holy Altra,
Polyeroatexist Birthology Rep-Ta-Meets; Air, water, Fruit, vegetables.

These are all of the qualities of every being and thing of GOD.   AMEN.

The seminar consists of OBS. and the Ultrapolyexistcreatologies or Altrapolyexistcreatalogies.   AMEN.

NOTE:

The Ghosts and Holy Ghost (Holy spirits) are of the Ultrapolyexistcreat-ologies and Ultrapolyexistcreatrons. They can and shall appear to be visible in visible, metaphysical, spiritual, physical and ultrapolyexistcreatological many places everywhere.   AMEN.

THE POWER OF GOD

The powers of God and of Idomiology.

God creates and recreates dependently, independently, directly
and indirectly, near or very far; God shall create God himself
finite or infinitively of whatever creation desired.

God also shall non create God such as non creatology or no
creatology of God himself of such desire to be a nothing at all or
of others than the Ultrapolyexistcreatologies.

NOTE: Ultraexistcreatology is a universal religion, education,
law, art, philosophy, science organization of God.   Amen.

NOTE: Furthermore, non creatology means no creation at all of God
Also, anti creatology means against creations of God. Amen.

The subject and object of Ultraexistcreatology is designed for people who are interested to accept and believe in what is of Ultraexistcreatology, but also not only to believe, but to acknowledge and to discipline oneself to comprehend as well as life goes among us.

The nature of this test is to see that the students meet the right requirements of comprehension for the examination of Ultraexistcreatology prescribed by the Ultraexistcreatologist.

A. J. Ultraexistcreatologist

This course of science of Ultraexistcreatology is designed for people who are interested in this type of religious educational science and philosophical science of God.   Amen.

For people who are not interested or do not accept this course of Science (Ultraexistcreatology) as being or can not meet the challenge or requirements or fit the needs of this course, then may I suggest and please advise you or them to find interest in or of some other Religion, Education, law, art, philosophy and science (field of prayer and study) etcetera.

This test is designed for people who are actually prepared, aware, and who do acknowledge this type of phenomena (Science of God) of God.

Thank you,

Courtesy of an Ultraexistcreatolo

A. J. Williams

The Purpose of this science is to show you how I penetrated the different levels, concepts, descriptions, definition and logics of my term the Introduction of Ultraexistcreatology (originally called the Introduction of the Ultrapolyexistcreatologies).

When reading this book you may not probably learn, interpret, conceive, understand. or penetrate this knowledge (known as certain powers of God), as slow or fast as you seem to think you can do or to be. First of all learning this science will take probably many devoted months and even years to actually get or sense the full Introduction of Ultraexistcreatology, etcetera. Amen.

Note: The Ultraexistcreatologists and ultraexistcreatology is actually the Religion, Education, Law, Art, Philosophy, Science, Organization of self and God, etcetera. Amen.

Note: The Introduction of Ultraexistcreatology is also conceived of Obsreptameets and R.E.L.A.P.S.O. of God.

Furthermore, Idomeology means, when God first knew or thought of creation such as us, etcetera. After God himself of the Ultrapoly-existcreatologies. Amen. Meaning we were thought of as a spirit without form until we became created by God, then God created us to be of another type of spiritual being (physical being). God thought of us as a spirit - then God created us physically.

God thinks spiritually to create spiritually. Amen.

The thought of God can be spiritual and physical (ultraexistcreato-logical). There are also an infinitive among Ghosts and Spirits (physical bodies) of the Ultrapolyexistcreatologies. Amen.

The nature in taking and passing this course is the recommendation of being awarded a certificate (degree) of approvals of your Professor, etcetera.

This is the actual certificate for graduation involving and taking the course from the Introduction of Ultraexistcreatology.

The nature of this course of R.E.L.A.P.S. is to acknowledge that this course only teaches you to learn the Religion, Education, Law, Art, Philosophy and Science of God and God's creations.   Amen.

The nature of this course is of (seminars) R.E.L.A.P.S.O.T.is to be acknowledged of this course which only teaches you and all to learn the Religion, Education, Law, Art, Philosophy, Science and organization of GOD and other than GOD'S creations, etcetera.   AMEN.

The nature in taking and passing this course is the recommendation of being awarded the certificates (degrees of approvals of your or our Professors, etcetera.   AMEN.

Involving those whom we graduate from the course or courses of Religion, Education, Law, Art, Philosophy, Science, Organization of this type of discipline, then we shall also be acknowledged of the field and fields of which we shall be awarded of these types of certificates (degrees) within and around us of GOD.   AMEN.

After completion then you shall be awarded the degrees of, and in Religion, Education, Law, Art, Philosophy, Science, organization of just taking the course or courses of Ultraexistcreatology.

Traditionally, you are to pass all your assignments of taking the course or courses and to be given all your degrees of what you accomplished here. and there of the Ultraexistcreatologists. Such as if you as a student or pupil pass the Relapsotherapy and test then you shall be awarded in all of your fields of accomplishments, such as a degree for every prayer and study you did of Religion, Education, Law, Art, Philosophy, Science, organization, Therapy testing R.E.L.A.P.S.O.T.T.

A degree for every course you take as a student shall pass of the Introduction of the Ultrapolyexistcreatologies.   AMEN.

Registration for the course of Ultraexistcreatology.

Please print correctly.

Name   Address   Phone

THE RELIGION OF ULTRAEXISTCREATOLOGY

This is to certify that

_____

has been awarded an Ultraexistcreatologist Degree on this day

_____, of recognition upon Completion of a Course

of Instruction by the Founder of Ultraexistcreatology.

Professor: _____

Graduate: _____

U

THE EDUCATION OF ULTRAEXISTCREATOLOGY

This is to certify that _____

has been awarded an Ultraexistcreatologist Degree on this day

_____ , in recognition upon Completion of a

COURSE OF INSTRUCTION by the Founder of Ultraexistcreatology.

PROFESSOR: _____

GRADUATE: _____

THE LAW OF ULTRAEXISTCREATOLOGY

This is to certify that _____

has been awarded an Ultraexistcreatologist Degree on this day

_____, in recognition upon Completion

of a Course of Instruction by the Founder of Ultraexistcreatology.

PROFESSOR: _____

GRADUATE: _____

U

THE ART OF ULTRAEXISTCREATOLOGY

This is to certify that _____

has been awarded an Ultraexistcreatologist Degree on this day of

_____ , in recognition upon Completion

of a Course of Instruction by the Founder of Ultraexistcreatology.

GRADUATE: _____

PROFESSOR: _____

U

THE PHILOSOPHY OF ULTRAEXISTCREATOLOGY .

This is to certify that _____

has been awarded an Ultraexistcreatologist Degree this day _____

_____ , of recognition upon Completion of a Course, of

Instruction by the Founder of Ultraexistcreatology.

Professor: _____

Graduate: _____

THE SCIENCE OF ULTRAEXISTCREATOLOGY

This is to certify that _____

has been awarded an Ultraexistcreatologist Degree on this day of

_____, in recognition upon Completion of a

Course of Instruction by the Founder of Ultraexistcreatology.

PROFESSOR: _____

GRADUATE: _____

THE ORGANIZATION OF ULTRAEXISTCREATOLOGY

(U)

This is to certify that _____

has been awarded an Ultraexistcreatologist Degree on this day of

_____, in recognition upon Completion of a

Course of Instruction by the Founder of Ultraexistcreatology.

PROFESSOR: _____

GRADUATE: _____

10>

THE THERAPY OF ULTRAEXISTCREATOLOGY

This is to certify that _____

has been awarded an Ultraexistcreatologist Degree on this day of

_____, in recognition upon Completion of

a Course of Instruction by the Founder of Ultraexistcreatology.

PROFESSOR: _____

GRADUATE: _____

Spiritual Enlightment of Obirthologod.   Introduction of Ultraexistcreatology

The testimony of Heaven/hell of obirthogod.   All souls regardless of what type of creation to be as long as in Obirthologod's heart you/I do rightousness shall go to see/live to dwell in the heavens with our Obirthologod after this life/death experiance.

Now those whom do not follow the universal christians religion, education, law, art, philosophy, science, organization and therapy shall not go to heaven but, to dwell in hell forever.

But our universe is hopeless/helpless being controlled by Devilish Gods consientiously, sub-conscientiously, and unconscienciously following Devilish Gods, amen.   Pray that the devils donot take our souls to God, amen.

Ultraexistcreatology of Obirthologods.

In the begining of Obirthologod and other Obirthologods have always been here before creation of the after/before like life/others like us. Obirthologods traveling around/in the Ultrapolyexistcreatologies in general creating all kinds of creatifications finite, infinite, destructible, in destructible, foreverlasting, and non-foreverlasting creations (Obirthologistifications) where ever/forever Obirthologods plan to do/be. Amen

After Obirthologods begining we (life of our particular creations became but, there where creations before us after Obirthologods) creatings in creation. Amen.

The creations before us after Obirthologods creations un-naturally died also as what is happening to us since the begining after Obirthologod's creations. Amen. We must pray/study Obirthologods creatifications:

Natural Predeterminants By Law of Obirthologod(s). Amen

Air, Water, Fruits, Vegetables, Mates: Male/female babies suck from their mother's nipples. Bathe in the morning, afternoon showers of rain and of either side n/s. Sleep at night all species and other laws like wise all life have a right to live.

Un-natural Predetermenants Deathologies eating of flesh of an animal or animals insects, creatures as wrong eating one another. Drinking or taking milk from any animal or animals and drinking it etc. lies, lying/killing trees/plants.

From the Obirthologod their are two opposite equally sexual offsprings of each species of the beginning and on other plants similar/non similar to each other (life). Amen.

Obirthologods (also moon/stars in syllabication-means Obirthologod) Amen

IF-SF-MF-FF-Thumbs

IT-ST-MT-FT-large toes   syllabication of paragons

U.C.R.E.-L.A.P.-S.O.-Therapy (Syllabication meanings)
Large Thumbs/toes and in sequence the others (fingers/toes)

The proper pronounciation (symbol/paradigme) according to these vocabulary of the hand/feet. First baby finger of the hand/foot; (O) Second finger of the right hand and second toe of the right foot: (birth) Middle finger/toe of the right hand/foot: (tho) fourth finger/toe of the right hand/right foot: (lo) thumb/large toe of the right hand/right foot: (Gy or God). Singular and plural -written as: Obirthology or Obirthologod, Obirthologies or Obirthologods. Amen.

The Universal Christians Religion, education, law, art, philosophy, science, organization, and therapy are also of the hands/feet; the thumbs/large toes either way represents Univeral Christians and the fingers and small toes in sequence represents R-E-L-A-P-S-O. therapy. Amen

A Divine Revelation/Speculation of an Ultraexistcreatological Heavenly Spiritual Site of Symbolical Formed Stars: Also, once ago shown the same meaning, but of the clouds formation the U/t =

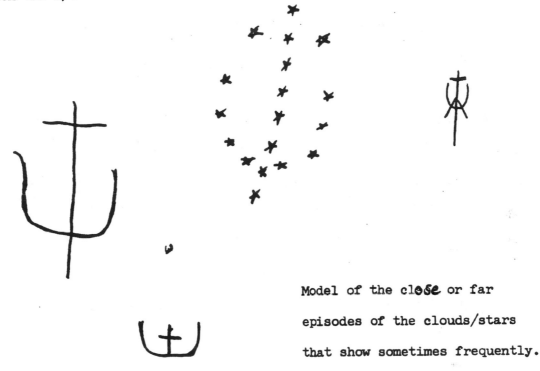

Model of the close or far episodes of the clouds/stars that show sometimes frequently.

Also the insights about the Introduction of Ultraexistcreatology (Obirthology of Obirthologods) Amen.

This is the representation of the Universal/Christians Religion, Education, Law, Art, Philosophy, Science, Organization, and Therapy of Obirthologod(s). Amen

The OBs Schools/Systems

Obirthologisticalization (Air, water, fruits, vegetables)

Obirthologisticalizations, Obirthologisticisms, Obirtholocies , *Birthology, (moon)*

Obirthologicalizations, Obirthrosities, Obirthoriums

Obirthorions, Obirthorizations, *Birthologitifications, OBirthologjes (Stars)*

Obirtholoverses (after/before

Universes, indestructable/destructible, foreverlasting/nonforeverlasting universes)

Obirtholum polars (Sun/planets only during the day to be *seemby the* sun, but has became

reversed *by* Devilish Gods to be seen at night with un-natural creatifications. Amen

Obirthrosities (powers: natural/unnatural)

Obirtholocy/Obirtholocies (powers also)

Obirthologod/Obirthologods: Referred to plato's republic.

Obirthorious, Obirthrons, Obirthroni-is

Obirthorian/Obirthoria (Ultrabioexistcreatology)

Obirthorians/Obirthorias (Ultrapolyexistcreatology) etc. also.

Why Did God Created and Creates Us?

Did we ask to come here or were we forced of creation
to come here of God? Was this one of God's evil doings to
force creation to face destruction such as us?

We did not ask God to create us. God creates and created
us to be or not to be.

The reason why God created or creates us, because God
is only of the ultrapolyexistcreatologies which means God
can only create and recreate of his own (with out life and
with out death) powers of his own formless or formful spirits.
God can create himself from one existence of creation to
another (of any creation desired).

What about the Devil? Does he create, recreate, and
destroy?

Yes, the Devil has similar powers from God and evil
powers which are not of God. Such as the serpent in the
Garden of Eden who tempted Eve to eat the forbidden fruit,
the apple of God.

Or is the Devil of God or not of God meaning did God
create a God who became the Devil; or is the Devil the Devil
which have been here also of the ultrapolyexistcreatologies;
or did God created himself to do evil; or did God created
the Devil or is it the Devil which have been here since God
which also gives an evil effect?

Yes of this Philosophical science shows whatever to be

or not to be does exist--to create etc. Meaning the family roots of God and the Devil does effects our planet and universe (Gods and Devils).

Ultraexistcreatology also means, the after and before infinitive all true beyond existence of creation of God.

The nature of the mind of ultraexistcreatology.

Physically we are here together, but mentally we are very far apart from one another of God.

Physically we are here together and mentally we are here together of God. As life gets worse we may seem to think that life gets better.

The attribution of Ultraexistcreatology.

The attribution of Ultraexistcreatology is to explain, explore, provide, research, detect, reasoning, comprehension, and lecture of all types of creations. To inform and direct theorist and scientist and others of profession that Ultraexistcreatology is the definite infinitive science which provides knowledge to be of examination, test speculation, research and observation of all types of creations of God and not of God.

Also, the attributes of Ultraexistcreatology is to sense within and around the beyond existence of creation or other than the beyond existence of creation. Such as God can, and do create various ways as the Ultraexist-creatology or Existcreatology which means God creates the beyond or not the beyond at all of various ways.

Furthermore, creatology, ultracreatology, existcreatology, ultraexist-creatology, ultrabioexistcreatology, and ultrapolyexistcreatology are all unlike in meaning, power, and creation of God. Each of the words means different as a degree and level of power of God. Also, as an Ultraexistcreat-ologist, God tells me that the first six concepts means what God created of our hands and palms to be acknowledged of such as the baby finger means creatology the second finger means Ultracreatology, the palm means exist-creatology, the middle finger means ultraexistcreatology, index finger means Ultrabioexistcreatology, and the thumb means Ultrapolyexistcreatology. An example of the fingers, palm, and thumb:

Ultrabioexistcreatology –
    Fifth – Index Finger

Ultrapolyexistcreatology –
    Sixth – Thumb

- ultraexistcreatology – 4th
                        finger

- ultracreatology - 2nd finger

- creatology - 1st finger

- existcreatology - 3rd - Palm

NOTE: Science from an ultraexistcreatological point of view means (SCI) - sight or

Knowledge (en) in what we sense or (ce) see.

Furthermore, the origination of Ultraexistcreatology became of and from

God who acknowledges the Ultrapolyexistcreatologies, etcetera. Amen.

The baby finger means creatology, the second finger means ultracreatology, the palm means existcreatology, the middle finger means ultraexistcreatology, the index finger means ultrabioexistcreatology, and the thumb means ultra-polyexistcreatology. An example of the fingers, palm and thumb:

Ultrabioexistcreatology   - Ultraexistcreatology fourth finger

Fifth finger .   - Ultracreatology   second finger

ultrapolyexistcreatology   - creatology first finger

sixth thumb   - existcreatology third palm

NOTE: Science from an ultraexistcreatological point of view means (SCI) -

              sight or knowledge (EN) in what we sense or (CE) see.

The appearance of God of the Ultrapolyexistcreatology.

God in perception is a spirit with or without form of infinity or finite
powers of himself.

God is a being of many finitive and infinitive powers, senses, such as
many eyes to see, many ears to hear, many mouths to speak, many minds
to think, many bodies to be, many creativities to enjoy, many colors to
create, many spirits to project, and many lives to live, many hands to
manipulate, many feet to travel, many wings to fly, and many finite and
infinitive sizes and weights to move and carry of God himself to live
upon being, but unlike us of our being of the Ultrapolyexistcreatrons of
God. Amen.

NOTE: God and life like us are of and consist of powers, meaning
Ultrapolyexistcreatrons also of others (generally), but unlike God's
Ultrapolyexistcreatrons, etcetera. Amen.

THE   CHARACTERISTICS

The left and right hands and feet representation in accordance to
syllabication of God's word and vocabulary of O-Come-Hap-Cebi-o-us-rep-ta-τ
which means, O I say O Come O I Lovegetables   O I say o come holy
Altrapolycreatexistbirthology, religion, education, preacher, teacher,
association, meets.

A diagram below of the ten syllables representing God's name, power,
of the hands and feet being etcetera. Amen.

NOTE: God creates the same of logic or the opposite of logic.

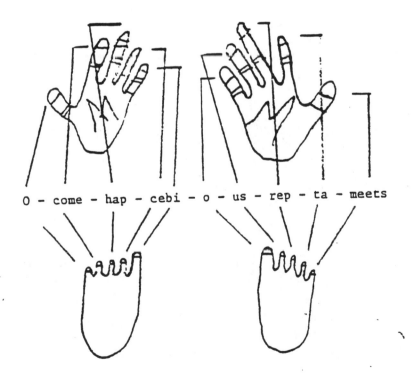

O - come - hap - cebi - o - us - rep - ta - meets

O – Come-hap – Cebi – O – Us – rep – ta – meets.

NOTE: Poly means many and O come hapcebiousreptameets means, O I say O come have happen and been sent by all of us, religion, education, preacher, teacher, association meets, ... bio .(from fifth and sixth syllables) of God's word and power as I mentioned above this paradigm means two types of creation, also of God such as the right and left hand, eyes, nose, also feet, ears, male and female, and the Sun and the Moon, etcetera. Amen.

Starting from the right hand representation of Idomeology:

The first finger means I

The second finger means DO

The Palm (third) means ME

The middle finger (fourth) means O

The index finger (fifth) means, LO

and the Thumb (sixth) means GY.

Idomiology means God creates and created others besides God himself and others besides God himself which God has not created, but only recognized, meaning there are others besides God himself, and our creation.

An example of the Left Hand representation:

Fifth index finger
(LO)

Sixth-thumb (GY)

Fourth finger (O)

Second finger (DO)

First finger (I)

Third - Palm - (MI)

(A Left Hand paradigm).

(1) = I, (2) = DO, (3) = MI, (4) = O, (5) = LO, (6) = GY.

Ocomehapcebiousreptameets and obsreptameets meaning, O I Say O come o
I Lovegetables O I Say O come Holy Altra poly createxistbirthology,
religion, education, preacher, teacher, association, meets, and R.E.L.A.P.S.O
meaning Religion, Education, Law, Art, Philosophy, as well as Science and
organization of the Ultrapolyexistcreatologies, God, etcetera. Amen.

Note: An Ultraexistcreatologist or Ultrapolyexistcreatologists means
 to sense the purification of divine love for God and God's creations,
etcetera. Amen.

To have you as a class apart of the student class graduate government (creation of God) is only to greet, meet, and inform you of what
you were unconscientiously acknowledging the Introduction of Ultraexistcreatology, until after you realized this phenomena. Amen.

Thank you for your attention and support of being here.

Sincerely yours,

A.J. Ultraexistcreatologist

Ultraexistcreatologist

A.J. Ultraexistcreatologist

NOTE: Ultraexistcreatology also means finite and infinitive existence
of God's creations and other than God's finite and infinitive
existence of creation.   Amen.

Starting from the right hand representation of Idomeology:

The first finger means I

The second finger means DO

The Palm (third) means ME

The middle finger (fourth) means O

The index finger (fifth) means, LO

and the Thumb (sixth) means GY.

Idomiology means God creates and created others besides God himself
and others besides God himself which God has not created, but only
recognized, meaning there are others besides God himself, and our creation.

An example of the Left Hand representation:

Fifth index finger
(LO)

Sixth-thumb (GY)

Fourth finger (O)

Second finger (DO)

First finger (I)

Third - Palm - (MI)

(A Left Hand paradigm).

(1) = I, (2) = DO, (3) = MI, (4) = O, (5) = LO, (6) = GY.

A representation of the right and left hand of Idomeology and
Idomiology in syllabications:

Starting from the right hand - Idomeology: means God always has been
here until God creates or created himself, and us, etcetera. A right hand
paradigm (top).

The first finger of the right hand means, I,

Second finger means, DO; the palm (third) means, ME

The (fourth) middle finger means, O; the index finger (fifth)
means, LO, and the thumb (sixth) means, GY.

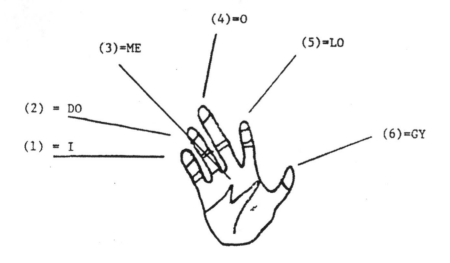

God's logic and quality of the Ultrapolyexistcreatology.

The logic of God is this God is God and we are of God. Man could not create himself unless he bccame God, because there is no evidence yet that man has power like God.

The logic also relates to quality meaning, God creates with given structure and character in his creations.

NOTE: God is the supreme being of the Ultrapolyexistcreatry (family roots of God) universal proof of God.   Amen.

Learn How to Question and Answer –

The Ultraexistcreatological mind and body.

Example:

To find the potential in one or many who may have the power

of God.

What are you creating in your mind? Meaning, what are you

thinking in or of your mind? What is your mind thinking or what are

you thinking in your mind? We are thinking and creating R.E.L.A.P.S.O.

of God's answer to Religion, Education, Law, Art, Philosophy, Science,

organizations. What is God thinking? God is thinking of O come

Hap cebiousreptameets, meaning, O I Say o come o I lovegetables

O I say o come have happen and been sent by all of us is also what

God and Creation thinks.   Amen.

Now all are of the un-natural universal
christians Mr-R.E.-L.A.P.-S.O.-Therapy
of Devilish God (s) also. Amen.

U.C.R.E.-L.A.P.-S.O.-Therapy of God/Gods. Amen.   Prayers for the

Ultrapolyexistcreatologies:

O I Say O come O I Lovegetables.

O I Say O come Hapcebious-Rep-Ta-meets; (TA:Tall), (REP: means REAP)

O I Say O come Have Happened and been sent by all of us. Religion Education
Preacher-Teacher Association Meets:

O I Say O come O I Lovegetables: Air, water, fruits/vegetables of Obirthologod/
Obirthologods names, powers/Glories.

O I Say O come - Holy - Altra - Poly - creat-exist-bious (Obirthologicalizations)
religion, Education, Preacher, Teacher-Association-meets:

O I Say O come O I Lovegetables O I Say O Come Hapcebious-Rep-Ta-meets.

Life is never alone of Obirthologod(s). of the great Magical Supreme beings.

we are never alone when we live or die.

Obirthologods shall always remember us of the pain/suffering we all continue to

go through and Obirthologods also shall pray for us as well as we shall pray for

Obirthologods. Amen.

This Intro-to Ultraexistcreatology shall provide you as a pupil with a sense

of direction as perception to observe intelligently about the Infinities throughout

the (Ultrapolyexistcreatologies) of Obirthologods. Amen. The book is a Divine Ritual

of circumstances: (Judgements for the Better/Worse of our life forms). Amen. Also,

outthere in space are Devilish Gods that causes un-happiness/casualties against us.

Amen.

ADDENDUM

From the Introduction of Ultraexistcreatology. Idomeology also means
that life (WE) were without life until God created us. Furthermore, we are
returning to where we - our life - was without life and without form,
Meaning A Spirit without life and death of God, etcetera. Amen.

Idomiology: means also when and where God creates or created life such
as the very first beginning to appear (the very first generation) to bear
their offsprings after them, etcetera.

The second generation after the first generation of God. Amen.

OBiRTHOLumpoIARS: Sun/pIANets only ─────── ─────────.

NOTE: Obirtholumpolars: means planets of God, also the stars and moon.

Obirtholumpolars: Sun play at day/all rest during night, the Sun/planets while
evolving there/here etc. Amen.

GOD: means, consist of Ultrapolyexistcreatrons and obsreptameetrons.

Ultrapolyexistcreatrons and obsreptameetrons means God's beyond existence
of creation of himself and other than God himself such as life like us and
other than God and ourselves (of various powers, levels, energies, characteristics
circuits, cells, etcetra. Amen.

ADDENDUM OF ULTRAEXISTCREATOLOGY

Idomeology: means, we were without form until God creates or created us. Amen.   Also means, the sun, God, etcetera.

Idomiology: means, the very first generation which brought forth the second generation. Amen.   Also means the Obirthologies (the moon and the stars, etcetera.).

O I Say O come O I Lovegetables O I Say O Come holy Altrapolycreatexistbirthologisticalizations, religion, education, preacher, teacher, association meets; Obsreptameets.

Obirthorians: Males among their kind of all species.

Obirthorias: Females among their kind of all species.

Obirthorious: Others among their kind and all of us; Obsreptamee

Obirtholumpalars: Means, (planets, the moons, stars, earths., sun)

Obirtholoverses: means, various or many universes of God and other than God's, etcetera. Amen.

Anticreatology: Means negative doings of the devils of creations

Non Creatology: Means, no creations at all such as positive, neutra, or negative, etcetera.

The syllabus of the instruction of Ultraexistcreatology.

First, the class shall learn the pronounciation of the vocabulary, meanings of the words, and their concepts, principles, logic, diagrams, paradigms, and origination of Ultraexistcreatology.

Second, the class will learn how to write, paraphrase and organize sentences and paragraphs pertaining to Ultraexistcreatology.

Third, I the Professor will read the subjects pertaining to Ultraexistcreatology.

Fourth, I shall teach what tools you need in order to support this science, et cetera.

Conclusion

To develop an university (college) first with the help
of the United States Government, and also to evacuate before
destruction of the earth and tie ourselves to live life more
effectively on a better planet as to conform and unite with
also our aliens or other than our aliens in space travels,
or to have God help us once we find our supreme being with
the tools which we manifest or to produce the equipment for
such given research such as high power telescopes and space
craft.

We could have done this a long time ago, but instead
only telephones, airplanes, cars and spaceships which could
never take you this or that far out towards planets only to
the moon a large star in the galaxy etcetera.

THE GLOSSARY OF ULTRAEXISTCREATOLOGY
(Self-Explanatory)

ALTRA: Means all true, ultimate and all true powers.

CREATOLOGY: Means the study of Creation or Creation of God.

DEVIL: Means an evil being with super powers which also creates
                and destroys.

EXISTCREATOLOGY: Means the study of the existence of GOD's creations.

GOD: Means a Supreme Being consisting of obsreptameets and
                ultrapolyexistcreatrons.

HOLY: Spiritual openings of powers of GOD such as mental, physical,
                and degree of characteristics as a whole or hole of the
                Universe. Also, means Closing of Powers.

IDOMEOLOGY: Means GOD always has been here until GOD creates or created
                GOD himself and others. Also means the Study of what GOD
                creates of GOD himself and why GOD has been as GOD is.

IDOMIOLOGY: Means GOD creates others and there are others besides GOD
                himself.

OBIRTHOLOGY: Means the moon and the stars at night. Also means the study
                of the moon and the stars, GOD, GOD's creations,etcetera.

OBSREPTAMEETS: Means and consists of what GOD and why GOD creates such as
                the definition and expression: O I say o Come O I Lovegetables
                o I say o Come Holy Altra-Polycreatexistbirthology, religion,
                education, preacher, teacher, Association meets.

Obirtholum-polars (sun/planets)

THE GLOSSARY (Continued)

OCOMEHAPCEBIOUSREPTAMEETS:

        Means also oI say o come o I lovegetables o I say o Come

        HOLY ALTRAPOLYCREATEXISTBIRTHOLOGY, religion, education,

        preacher, teacher, association, meets.

POLY: Means many of the total sum or infinity of GOD's creations,
            etcetera,

ULTRACREATOLOGY: Means the study of the beyond creation of GOD unlike
        Creatology of what GOD can or shall do. This is the second
        power of GOD according to our hands.

5TH FINGER = Ultrabioexistcreatology - Ultraexistcreatology - FOURTH FINGER

6TH THUMB = Ultrapolyexistcreatology - Ultracreatology - SECOND FINGER

                                - Creatology - FIRST FINGER

                                - Existcreatology - PALM 3RD INDICATIO

ULTRAEXISTCREATOLOGY:

        Means the study of the beyond existence of GOD's creations.

THE GLOSSARY (Continued)

ULTRAEXISTCREATOLOGIST:

> One and many of the profession who know the law, art, and
> Science of God. Amen.

ULTRABIOEXISTCREATOLOGY:

> Means study of the beyond two existences of God's two
> creations, such as male and female, or day and night.

ULTRAPOLYEXISTCREATOLOGY:

> Means the study beyond many existences of God's many
> creations.

ULTRAPOLYEXISTCREATOLOGISTS:

> Means the nature of God's creations of many professionals
> (divine) (Obsreptameets) who also know the law, art, and
> Science, etcetera.

ULTRAPOLYEXISTCREATRY:

> All roots and characteristics of the Universe (family trees).

ULTRAPOLYEXISTCREATIFICATIONS:

> Means the beyond many wonderful existences of God's many
> (Characteristics) Creations, such as beings, and things, etc.

THE GLOSSARY (Continued)

ULTRAPOLYEXISTCREATRONS:

      Means specifically and generally electrical energies of

      (In Beings and things) various conceptions, etcetera.

ULTRADOMES: Means where God and other ultrapolyexistcreations live.

VEGETABLES: Means most logical food consumed by man, animals, insects,

      creatures, trees, God and the beyond many existences of

      God's many creations. Also means lovegetables of this

      science are derived from O I Say o Come o Lovegetables

      o I Say o come Holy   Atrapolycreatexistbirthology, religion,

      education, preacher, teacher, association meets.